THE DUNMAGLASS CLAIM
LUCY AND JEAN

THE DUNMAGLASS CLAIM
LUCY AND JEAN

By Jane S. Macgillivray

First published in 2004 by

J. Macgillivray
4 Wyndham Mews
London W1H 2PN

www.dunmaglass.com

ISBN 0-9548749-0-0

Typeset and jacket design by A. Bougrine
www.choosealex.com

Printed and bound by Cox & Wyman Ltd, Reading

Omnia terrena per vices sunt aliena
Nunc mea nunc hujus, post mortem nescio cujus;
Nulli certa domus

***

All terrene things by turn we see
Become another's property;
Mine now, must be another's soon
I know not whose, when I am gone
An earthly house is bound to none

Inscription on wall of the old Kilravock town-house in Nairn,
known more recently as MacGillivray Buildings

CONTENTS

APPENDIX

AUTHOR'S NOTE

PEDIGREE TABLES

SOURCES

INDEX

ACKNOWLEDGEMENTS

I would like to express my gratitude for their patience, advice and help to Dr. David Sellar, Faculty of Law, University of Edinburgh, Dr. Edward Cashin, Center for the Study of Georgia History, Augusta State University, Dr. Harry Duckworth, University of Manitoba, Canada; their opinions and interpretation do not necessarily correspond to my own.

I am deeply indebted to Sally and Peter Mackintosh, formerly of Cradlehall, Inverness and Inverurie, who most generously made this research possible.

My thanks are due to Roy McGilvray, Canada, Robert McGillivray, Clan historian, Scott Coltrain, America, Marie Fraser of Fraser Association, Canada, Dr. Alan Macpherson, University of Newfoundland, Bill Lawson, Co Leis Thu?, Isle of Harris, Sr. Guillermo Delgado Brackenbury, Sevilla, Ian Davidson, Clan Davidson Association, Dr. A. W. Parker, University of Dundee, Lady Angelica Cawdor, William MacGillivray, Auldearn, Dr. John B. MacGillivray, Dundee, Alastair and Margaret Beattie, Alasdair McLeod, Inverness Library, the helpful team at the National Archives of Scotland in Edinburgh who have kindly given me permission to publish the letters quoted, also the teams at Inverness Archives and library, John and Jenny Rose-Miller, Cawdor Heritage Group, Jamie and the late Meta Scarlett, Moy, Scott Matthews, Australia, Tessa Malcolm, Australia, Alastair Watson, New Zealand and Alice Parte, Saint Germain en Laye, France. I have also been helped by many internet friends and fellow-researchers all over the world and to them go my thanks for their time and the information they provided.

Last but not least, my thanks for support and encouragement go to my mother Beatrice Macqueen Macgillivray, my brother John Macgillivray of London, the late Vladimir Bougrine and my children, Alexander, Camilla, and most especially Mary who graciously accompanied me to Inverness for a year and to whom with great affection I dedicate this book.

CHAPTER ONE
LITIGATION FOR DUNMAGLASS

Who were the heirs?

When John Lachlan, last of a long line of M'Gillivray chiefs, died heirless in Inverness in 1852, he left one year's rental to his tenants, who included half a dozen of his name, and some £30,000 to charity and his wife's relatives.[1] His main legatee was his long-term housekeeper, Charlotte Clark who, according to his will, should eventually be buried alongside him and his wife in the remote Highland cemetery at Dunlichity. There was surprised silence, then a clamour of claimants for John Lachlan's lands which had not been disposed of in his will. He had been the only wealthy chief of a small clan that for centuries eked a mean living from cattle-rearing in the Highlands. But the previous century, two relatives had ventured to the New World; they had made fortunes in Georgia and Florida and made him their heir. Who now were John Lachlan's own 'heirs-at-law'; who would inherit the lands? This was the issue in a 10-year litigation conducted in the Edinburgh courts, and when the awards were eventually made after a lengthy procedure, they appear to have gone to the wrong people.

The long-held entailed lands of Dunmaglass and its 17,000 acres in Strathnairn, as well as the properties of Wester Lairgs and the Easter half of Gask could go only to a male M'Gillivray, while the equally vast estates that had been bought more recently with the American fortunes - Faillie, Wester Gask, half of Inverernie and and Easter Aberchalder – would simply go to the nearest-of-kin, which could include descendants of a female M'Gillivray.

---

[1] The different ways of writing the name throughout the centuries - MacGillivray, McGill(i)vray, MackGillivray and M'Gillivray being the most common, with or without a capital G - have been standardised as M'Gillivray, the version adopted for the documents presented to the court. The variations depended on the scribe (even on brothers) and the period. Similarly, Mackintosh or McIntosh has been rendered M'Intosh.

John Lachlan had designated no heirs and apparently had no close M'Gillivray relations, so it was necessary to delve far back into the past to identify the nearest collateral branch with a male heir. The descendants of the 17th century brothers of John Lachlan's ancestor, Alexander, whose male line had now died out, competed in the lawcourts for Dunmaglass and the attendant chiefship of the M'Gillivray clan. The successful claimant would necessarily descend from the next younger brother of Alexander, for this is how the law of inheritance worked. So the question seemed straightforward: Who was older, Donald or William?

The M'Gillivrays in Lonnie and Canada

Several generations previously in the 17th century, Donald the Tutor and William, younger brothers of Alexander M'Farquhar[2] of Dunmaglass, had secured their future and status by becoming owners of the woodland estate of Dalcrombie, to the south of Inverness. One brother took the western portion, the other the eastern, and thus both became landed proprietors, and their families known as 'of Dalcrombie', although they may not actually have lived in these remote lands above Loch Duntelchaig. Donald the Tutor looked after the affairs of the two orphaned children of his older Dunmaglass brother and of his elderly father who outlived him.

Donald had several sons himself, the most successful of whom was Farquhar who had moved from the Highlands to live in Lonnie in Petty, described as the lowest-lying farmlands in Europe, stretching along the beaches of the Moray Firth. Farquhar was usually titled 'Aberchalder' rather than Dalcrombie, after an estate taken over from a M'Gillivray owner who failed to repay his debts. He was the family banker, co-financing bills, lending money, buying and selling cattle.[3] Most of the bonds or bills issued by Dunmaglass, or other members of the family, carry his name as cautioner or joint borrower. Yet like others at the time, he was never

---

[2] Alexander signed M'Farquhar, not M'Gillivray.

[3] He may have been the Farquhar who engaged in the 1715 rebellion, was taken prisoner and escaped.

solvent. Bailie John Steuart, the Earl of Moray's factor, had business with Aberchalder but wearied of his continually precarious finances.

Aberchalder's son, Donald in Torbreck, apparently married Janet M'Gillivray, his Dunmaglass second cousin, and took over the Lonnie farmhouse when his father died in 1733, at about the same time as two of his cousins.[4] Donald found that much money was owing to his father, and promptly sued the wives and children of his deceased relations for repayment. Donald did not engage in the second Jacobite rebellion, but was killed for his clothes by dragoons the day after the battle of Culloden.

Donald's son Farquhar, born in the 1720s, moved from Lonnie back to the family property at Dalcrombie. From here he ran an illicit distillery, administered the Scottish estates of cousins in America, and acquired a reputation for being the most wicked and rapacious man in Inverness. He engaged in successive litigations of dubious tenor, designed to enrich his family at the expense of others. Despite his legal skill and profiteering, his children had to make their own way in the world.

Farquhar's only son who left issue was John. *The Dictionary of Canadian Biography* states he was born in 1770, the *Encyclopaedia of Canada* 1777[5] with a question mark; *The Inverness Courier* wrote that he died aged 84 in 1855 while his gravestone in Canada shows his birth as 1777. But there is little doubt about John's ancestry; when one of Farquhar's Dallas granddaughters moved to Canada, she was recognized as John's niece.

John moved to Canada and started working as a clerk in 1794 in the fur-trading North West Company that his relative William

---

[4] Aberchalder's younger son Alexander, who died at Culloden, farmed at Lonnie and married Margaret, daughter of Alexander M'Intosh of Borlum at Termit, a successful trader with England and the continent like Bailie Steuart. Daughters: Elizabeth married Robert of the other Dalcrombie family a short walk away at Dalzeil, Marjory married Thomas Fraser of Garthmore in 1729 and Marie may have married Thomas Fraser, son of Farraline.

[5] This could not be right; John witnessed a legal document with his brother Lachlan in 1787, an improbable duty for a ten-year-old. The *Encyclopedia* credits him with a brother Duncan and notes this Duncan is not to be confused with the brother of William of the NWC. Duncan does not appear in his father's will; he may have died by the time it was drawn up. 1771 is the year of birth of another John, brother of William of the North West Company in Canada; it is not known what became of him.

M'Gillivray had joined ten years previously, and like William, he had native children in the North West. When John was made a partner, an unkind contemporary commented that he was 'too slow and unfit to conduct an opposition' which may suggest that he was not as ruthless as some of his colleagues. He built a home in Williamstown, Glengarry County, Ontario and called it Dalcrombie. In 1816-17 he visited Britain with his young wife, Gaelic-speaking Isobel McLean. He received a small legacy from William M'Gillivray of the North West Company who described him as 'cousin' in his will. From 1839 to 41, he served on the Legislative Council of Upper Canada, and was known thereafter as the Honorable John M'Gillivray. When he retired from the Hudson's Bay Company, it was with a 'competent fortune' according to the *Inverness Courier*.

Although many in Scotland doubted he could produce evidence in support of his claim to one of the M'Gillivray properties, Easter Aberchalder, the Hon. John had kept a valuable document, an old notarised contract of sale that his father had negotiated with a reversion clause to his own line; if Dunmaglass had no descendants, this property would come to his father's branch of the family. The Canadian thus became the uncontested owner of Easter Aberchalder only months after John Lachlan's death. But a greater possession was Dunmaglass. The following year, Neil John presented the second petition received at the Sheriff of Chancery's offices 'praying to be served nearest and lawful heir-male to the deceased John Lachlan'. Legal procedure was slow, and the Hon. John died a year or two later, so his claim was taken up by eldest son, Neil John, born in 1827. Neil John's activities in Canada were clouded in rumours of financing, risky ventures and a bank that crashed. But the Canadian financier in his twenties was the most serious contender for Dunmaglass. He was the great-great-great-grandson of Donald the Tutor, the first M'Gillivray owner of Dalcrombie.

In the absence of any closer tie-in to the Dunmaglass family, Neil John's entitlement seemed undeniable. He was descended from a 'tutor', traditionally an orphaned child's oldest paternal uncle. As things stood, there did not seem to be much hope for the counter-claimant who descended from William, the other brother 'of Dalcrombie' who lived in the farm of Wester Lairgs near Moy.

The M'Gillivrays in Dalzeil, the Carolinas and Jamaica

This William of Dalcrombie had two sons, John and Donald. The latter remained in the remote Highlands near Dunmaglass and in turn had two sons, Lachlan and John. Lachlan was sent a prisoner after the 1715 rebellion to the Carolinas where he later became a trader. A registered will in Charles Town in 1733 shows that he had assets to leave to his father, brother and cousin Archibald. But there are no more records that show Donald's line.

William's son John married at least twice; his last wife, Janet M'Intosh, was sister to two successive clan chiefs. He lived next to his cousins, the Lonnie M'Gillivrays, on the handsome farmstead of Dalzeil and then Tullich, and appears to have led the same busy life of cattle-breeder and Inverness financier as his cousin Aberchalder, also conducting business with the Earl of Moray's factor, Bailie John Steuart, at nearby Castle Stuart.

He had several sons and daughters. According to descendants, his son Alexander was attainted in the lst Jacobite rebellion, and his half of the family property of Dalcrombie passed to the Lonnie cousins as being next of kin. In fact, Alexander's father John was still owner at this time, and was doing business with Bailie John Steuart at the end of 1716. The property seems to have changed hands after a straightforward sale several years later. But Alexander did end up in the Carolinas, and may have been sent there a prisoner, perhaps with his older brother William. Their brother Farquhar was still in Scotland in 1721, but reportedly died abroad. Did John of Dalcrombie visit his son or sons in America? Simon Fraser Mackintosh, who set out the genealogies of the M'Gillivray family in the 19th century, wrote (but then heavily crossed it out) that John worked in a Mercantile House in Carolina, where he resided some time before returning to Scotland. When John died in 1733 (we do not know where, but coincidentally at the same time as his nephew in America and his Lonnie cousin), his widow Janet M'Intosh was cited in a legal summons together with only two of her children, Robert and Anne. The other children had married and left home or were in America.

Alexander, described as of the Carolinas and a wealthy man, immediately returned to Scotland on his father's death, and married in 1736. He stayed for a while in Dalzeil, but brought up his children either in America or in Scotland, and at one time lived on the farm of Knocknagael, near Inverness. But it was Alexander's younger brother, Archibald, who developed with Alexander or inherited from his cousin Lachlan what in the 1730s was the largest trading company in the Carolinas. It had twenty pack-horsemen and one hundred and twenty three horses.[6] Their brother Robert, who had stayed in Scotland, married twice and looked after the farm of Dalzeil.[7] When the battle of Culloden raged at his doorstep, he died valiantly with the blood of many Hanoverians on his sword, and when the sword broke, he went on fighting with a cartwheel. Simon Fraser Mackintosh wrote that he was much the strongest man at Culloden.

Despite Archibald's success as a trader, he did not remain in Carolina, but followed Alexander back to Scotland, probably arriving in the middle of the rebellion. Another member of the clan, Lachlan, had taken his place in Charles Town and was starting out on a route that would lead to even greater success and wealth. Archibald had apparently come home to settle for he soon married Lucy, a daughter of the Kyllachy M'Intoshes and leased the farm of Daviot, near Inverness, from his uncle, the M'Intosh chief.

Archibald's ties with the New World remained strong: three sons, John, James and Lachlan, returned to America and worked for their relations. Lachlan took their slaves to Jamaica when the Loyalists had to leave. He is found here with one white dependant in 1786, and had two children aound the turn of the century, then returned briefly to Scotland in 1807 where he married Ann Kennedy, the daughter of an Inverness doctor. It was their son, another Lachlan, now in his forties, who was counter-claimant against the Canadian M'Gillivray.

Rev. Lachlan had come a long way for this inheritance, together with his family, and had now hired a pay-if-you-win lawyer. He was

---

[6] An early but older partner was Daniel Clark, who had also left the Dalzeil homestead for the Carolinas; yet another Dalzeil youth who came over was James Macqueen of Corrybrough

[7] He had issue but the names are not known. Daughter Ann, married to Hendry, was sole heir to her mother in 1805. Robert's sister Ann married Alexander M'Gillivray of Aberchalder and moved to that farm near Dunmaglass.

not displeased about returning to his homeland: in Australia, where he had emigrated as a young man and where he gave 'divine service', his principal and rather unsatisfactory occupation was as a minor civil servant. Against all odds, he judged his prospects to be brighter in Scotland.

It is surprising that Reverend Lachlan should have bothered to enter the fray. The Canadian claimed to descend from the brother known as 'the Tutor', who would take precedence over his own ancestor. In addition, as Reverend Lachlan himself admitted in his condescendence, one of the American relations had entailed Dunmaglass to Neil John's grandfather if John Lachlan had no issue.

Reverend Lachlan M'Gillivray was great-great-grandson of William of Wester Lairgs.[8]

A secret deal

There was a third claimant competing for Dunmaglass and its lands, but he did not stay in the running for very long. Alexander M'Gillivray was a labourer on the Urquhart estate of Patrick Grant, sheriff-substitute of Inverness and one of John Lachlan's trustees. Although first to enter his claim, he may never have been a real contender but rather the means to put Dunmaglass into the hands of a receiver, an office that his landlord's son soon occupied. Alexander's claim was later dropped. This is the only glimpse we have of him and nothing is known about his relationship to the Dunmaglass family.[9]

Although the case had taken years to prepare, the actual hearings in 1857 in Edinburgh were brief. The jury was supposed to decide which was the elder of the two brothers born in the 17th

---

[8] He presented himself as the eldest son of Lachlan of Sunflower Estate, Jamaica, youngest son leaving issue of Archibald of Daviot, second son leaving issue of John, portioner of Dalcrombie (the male descendants of Robert being extinct, the sons of the first marriage of John died unmarried except his third son Alexander, who died leaving one son, John, who died in America unmarried and with no issue).

[9] The census shows he was 52 and born in Daviot; the closest Alexander in the old parish baptism records is the son of a Donald M'Gillivray and Ann M'Gillivray, born in 1797, with siblings Catherine and Margaret.

century, but the issue seemed rather to be who the late John Lachlan considered his heir. According to papers deposited by Neil John's lawyers at the National Archives of Scotland, there was a jury of twelve - a grocer, tailor, veterinary surgeon, spirit dealer, druggist, dairymaid, two boot makers, farmers and engravers - none of whom bore a Highland name. They must have eyed these Scots from abroad with astonishment and curiosity. Although they were inexperienced in matters of clan genealogy, their job was to listen to elderly Gaelic-speaking witnesses and choose 'the nearest and lawful heir-male of John Lachlan M'Gillivray of Dunmaglass, deceased'. *The Inverness Courier* reported:

> 'Many of the witnesses being veteran Highlanders, aged from seventy to eighty years, considerable difficulty existed in eliciting answers. The Reverend T. M'Lachlan, of the Gaelic church, attended as interpreter. But whenever the witnesses knew any English at all, the Court requested them to answer directly in that language, apparently repugnant though it was to them. Some of the replies thus given to questions imperfectly understood created great merriment in Court. One old farmer having been asked his age, he said about seventy. How long is it since your mother died? Fifteen years ago. How old was she? Between forty and fifty – (Laughter. The witness was thus older than his mother before her death). Do you mind the date of your father's death? - Not exactly; I took no notice of it. (Great laughter)'

The proceedings are described differently in three typewritten pages deposited at the Lyon's Office in Edinburgh. No source is cited, but they seem to be extracts from a book, now lost, supposedly in the possession of Neil John's son when he died. According to these pages, the Canadian Neil John had powerful support for his claim: that of Aeneas M'Intosh, brother to the chief, also from Canada. Aeneas' uncle had been involved in a similar inheritance case in 1820 on his return from Jamaica. To prove his claim to the M'Intosh lands, he had produced elderly witnesses who remembered his father's pedigree. Now Aeneas recalled his conversations with John Lachlan, his riding companion; they were both 'fond of horses'.

'I was in the way of visiting him, and was very intimate with him. He frequently spoke about his heir in the years 1840 to 1850;

he said he was in America, that it was one of the Dalcrombie family – he had no near relatives in this country.'

Another witness was Mary M'Intosh, niece of the late Provost John of Inverness, and second cousin to Rev. Lachlan. Despite this connection, she gave evidence that was prejudicial to his cause: 'I am daughter of the late Charles M'Intosh, W.S. He died in 1818. He was seventy-two years of age. He had charge of Dunmaglass property. I have often seen John Lachlan, the late proprietor. I never heard of any person acting for Dunmaglass but my father. (…) I recollect seeing a relative of his coming from Canada. It was young M'Gillivray of Dalcrombie. (…) I have heard my father say that he was astonished that Dunmaglass could let him go away. My father thought that Dalcrombie was next heir. He regretted that Dunmaglass had no heir, and that Dalcrombie was heir. I paid little attention at the time. I have heard my father repeatedly talking in that way. I heard others talking in the same way.'

The third witness that Neil John cited was Lachlan M'Intosh, who was agent for some of the heirs-female in the litigation for different M'Gillivray lands. He confirmed that his research showed there were no male heirs who were closer than Neil John.

Eight other witnesses were examined for Neil John, including three of the name M'Gillivray; their ages ranged from sixty four to seventy two. Sadly what they said was not noted. Five more witnesses were cited, but not examined.

Rev. Lachlan's papers have been printed in bookform and are held in the Charles Fraser-Mackintosh Collection at Inverness Library. They include old family letters, a letter from one of John Lachlan's curators, and two wills that we shall see later. In his condescendence to the court, Rev. Lachlan admitted that Colonel John, one of the wealthy M'Gillivrays his father had worked for, had executed a disposition and conveyance of the properties in favour of Neil John's grandfather if the Dunmaglass line failed, and this decreet of adjudication had been properly recorded in the Record of Abbreviates in 1787. But Rev. Lachlan claimed that Colonel John had done this without having acquired any title to the estates.

Two years previously, Rev. Lachlan's lawyer Thomas Thomson had concluded that Farquhar of Aberchalder's legitimacy was questionable, and more importantly that Donald the Tutor was older than William, Rev. Lachlan's ancestor. Thomson then wrote: "The weakest part of the case is the evidence that Donald and William were sons of Farquhar McAllister but that applies to your case as well as your opponent's ....Were I in your situation I would give up the case as hopeless; it is so in every sense as I am sure I have exhausted all the sources of proof and got not a single fact in favour of your claim."

But something had come up to make him change his mind, for both Rev. Lachlan and his lawyer had stayed the course. What Lachlan argued in court was not recorded although according to an early 20th century issue of *Celtic Monthly* he denied that Donald was the next eldest son, and attempted to cast doubt on the Hon. John's marriage in Canada. This was reported with some indignation: 'The Canadian marriage of Mr. Neil John M'Gillivray's father was fully established by witnesses who knew his father and mother; and the documentary proofs left no doubt as to Donald the Tutor's position in the pedigree.'

The court had difficulty understanding the Highland witnesses, who must have been distressed at the outbursts of mirth and hilarity their answers caused. Fortunately for them, this affront did not last long. On the very first day, there was a surprise recess in the proceedings. The two sets of lawyers retired, returning with a joint statement that Rev. Lachlan was withdrawing from the competition. What was not reported was that the claimants had in fact come to an arrangement whereby, in exchange for his withdrawal, Rev. Lachlan would receive financial compensation, namely the accumulated rent on Dunmaglass since John Lachlan's demise, which was estimated at about £3,000. Rev. Lachlan's lawyer would later refer to the research he had undertaken and the skilful use he had made of this at the trial, which had resulted in this prize.

We do not know what the lawyer and Rev. Lachlan's £3000 trump card was, and whether the witnesses themselves were a real liability for the claimants. Whatever Thomson had unearthed, it wouldn't win his client the case. But given the all the evidence showing that Neil John had by far the stronger case, it was clearly significant enough to prejudice his total success.

The witnesses were dismissed. Now all the jury had to do was pronounce on the accuracy of Neil John's ancestry. The latter was duly found acceptable and, the claim being uncontested, Neil John became heir to Dunmaglass, Wester Lairgs and the Easter half of Gask, as well as chief of the M'Gillivray clan.

'Let the lawyers say what they would'

When the Canadian laird finally set foot on his remote lands in the autumn of 1858, there was great rejoicing. His tenants and neighbours prepared a banquet, danced and toasted him all night because Neil John was the better option; for some reason, they had not wanted Reverend Lachlan to succeed. The lawyers though voiced doubts about the outcome; they did not believe that Neil John was the true heir to Dunmaglass and Wester Lairgs.

The Inverness Courier reported that the dinner and ball was a great success. Below are extracts:

'(Neil John's) accession to the estate gave sincere satisfaction in Dunmaglass, where Mr. MacGillivray was to some extent personally known and whither very favourable reports of his character and disposition had preceded him. In order that all might have an opportunity of meeting him and in order also that they might show respect to the heir of the Dunmaglass family, the tenantry on the estate invited Mr. MacGillivray to a dinner at the Mains farm, which took place on Friday last. The day was fine, and besides the tenantry, many other friends of Mr. MacGillivray were present. On his approach to the Mains, some 200 persons met the carriage and having unyoked the horses, they dragged the vehicle to the scene of the banquet, preceded by pipers and loudly cheering all the way. Materials for a large bonfire had been previously collected on the top of Mamour and towards evening a large party assembled around the pile which they set on fire; and having drunk to the health and prosperity of the laird, they danced around the fire, then returned to join the dinner party. (...) After dinner and toasts to the Queen, the Prince Consort, the rest of the family, the Army and the Navy, Mackintosh of Mackintosh, the chairman called for a special bumper to the health of their esteemed guest - the laird.

We have met, he said, to give a welcome to Mr. MacGillivray on his arrival in our country, to take up his abode on the estate of his ancestry, and I am sure I speak the sentiments of all when I say that he receives a most sincere and hearty welcome. Neither he nor his family are strangers to us, and many an anxious wish during the litigation did we all express that he should be, as I rejoice to say he is, now among us. We felt satisfied, *let the lawyers say what they would, and let the issue be what it might*, that our honoured guest was the true heir of Dunmaglass and no other could have received a hearty welcome or been acknowledged as our chief.

I would not in the presence of Mr MacGillivray expatiate on his many virtues, but I may be permitted to say that from all we have seen and known of him, as well as from what we have learnt regarding him, he will be a good and honoured landlord. *He has sprung from a good stock.*[10] His father and mother had been well-known to the tenants, and had been as universally esteemed as known: and I doubt not the Laird will keep alive those pleasing recollections of the parents.

The chairman concluded by calling on the company to join him in wishing Mr MacGillivray long life, health and happiness in the enjoyment of his property. The toast was drunk with Highland honours, and immense cheering.'

The young Canadian from Williamstown was very flattered. When it was his turn to speak, he declared: 'I fear I shall not be able to realize all your high expectations regarding me, but the honour which you have done to me today as well as former kindnesses shown to my family, will impel me to do my duty; and if I am not as

---

[10] Our italics

good a landlord as your hopes lead you to expect, believe me the fault will be of the head and not of the heart.'

Parts of the newspaper report are astonishing: 'He has sprung from good stock.' Yet an Inverness worthy, Mr. Fraser-Tytler, would later write that Neil John's grandfather was a murderer who had fled to Canada, the MacGillivray clan book that he was arrogant, callous and cruel, and Charles Fraser-Mackintosh, 19th century historian and Member of Parliament, that he was the most wicked man in Inverness together with Macpherson in Ballachroan. Perhaps there was more to Neil John's ancestry than meets the eye, but as the welcome-home speech made clear: 'Let the lawyers say what they would, and let the issue be what it might - our honoured guest (Neil John) is the true heir of Dunmaglass!'

What had the lawyers been saying? Who did they think was the true heir? Was Neil John's lawyer among those who doubted the legitimacy of the outcome? What was the complication that led the chairman of the evening's celebrations to declare: 'Let the issue be what it might...' These were not questions at the time. The answers were known to the whole company assembled at Dunmaglass that night, and to the readers of the *Inverness Courier* also, but not to a single soul today.

Despite Neil John's good resolutions, charm, 'good stock' and being a far better Highlander than his predecessor - the last of the old line, as the *Celtic Monthly* described John Lachlan - Neil John had no head for business or for running an estate as he himself admitted. The court case and settlement had been costly, and although he drank and danced, he had already sown the seeds of his own destruction. His mounting debts would mean the end of the M'Gillivray possessions in Strathnairn. Very soon the lands that had been home to the Scottish clan for centuries would be fully mortgaged and irretrievably lost.

CHAPTER TWO
DELVING INTO THE PAST

Farquhar of Dunmaglass and his brother William, the 'Captain Ban'

Half the inheritance - the half that was entailed to a male heir that also carried the chiefship of the clan - had been allotted, but there remained the lands of Faillie, Wester Gask and Invererny that were not entailed and could be claimed by the nearest heir (not necessarily a male or a M'Gillivray). Here there were more recent connections to the Dunmaglass family that we shall now outline.

Farquhar of Dunmaglass, the nephew of Donald and William whose descendants claimed the estate in the 19th century, was head of the clan at the end of the 17th century. He fought in the last clan battle at Mulroy in 1688, when the M'Intoshes were humiliated by the MacDonells. Numerous kinsmen farmed in the hills and glens: Donald in Tulloch, Lachlan in Cullnagaig, a couple of Beans, Thomas, Thomas Dow and his son William, Farquhar MackAllaster vic Padrick and Malcolm in Dunmaglass, another in Dalcrombie, Donald in Flichity, Donald of Aberchalder - a jumble of M'Gillivrays whose names have come down to us mostly through the Register of Hornings and Books of Adjournal, where their names were recorded for unpaid debts or crimes such as trespassing on others' lands.

Farquhar's sister Margaret married twice; her husbands were William Fraser of Meikle Garth and Alexander Macpherson of Crubenmore and Breakachie. Farquhar, married to Emilia Steuart of Newtown, was Commissioner of Supply for Inverness, which meant he collected land taxes, paid for schools and the upkeep of roads. The laird of M'Intosh, Member of Parliament for Inverness, had probably secured the appointment for him.

Farquhar and Emilia's children were Farquhar, William, alias the 'Captain Ban' (i.e. 'white'[11]), Donald and David, and daughters were Anna, Janet[12] and perhaps Magdalene[13]. The family appears to have lived at the farm at Gask, surrounded by a thick copse of tall trees, on the shortest route from Strathnairn into Inverness, scarcely six miles from town. It was a modest farmhouse by any standards, with thick wattle walls, a large fireplace in a small room, an adjoining byre for the cattle, and a couple of rooms above; a very simple abode for a Highland chief that could not rival the Dalcrombie's farmstead of Dalzeil. It still stands today, alone and remote, but at the time it would have been at the centre of a hamlet.

A close and powerful presence in the parish of Daviot and Dunlichity was the Jacobite Mister or Magister Michael Fraser, an extraordinary man of the church, more interested in art, literature and politics than moral indictment and holy ritual. His eccentricity included painting and continual absence from the parish, which quickly endeared him to his congregation. His second wife was from this close-knit community: Elizabeth, daughter of the neighbouring M'Beans at Faillie or Kinchyle. Of Fraser's children by his second marriage, we must mention Isobel who would marry the tall, handsome Highlander neighbour, John, natural son of William, the Captain Ban.[14]

Rebellion loomed after the Act of Union which was hated by Highland chiefs and welcomed by the Whigs in Inverness. The senior Farquhar did not live long enough to see his sons engage with the Jacobite forces. To these young men, there was a threefold call to arms: from Fraser, their spiritual guide, who considered the Stuart monarchs to be Scotland's rulers by divine right; from Sir Hugh Campbell, their feudal superior, who saw Scotland's future as an

---

[11] 'White' is assumed to refer to his complexion, although in the Nairnwhire fairy-tale he has the role of a white knight.

[12] Sources: Farr Manuscript and litigation claim by a descendant of Donald of Dalcrombie. There is no documentary evidence. There may have been other children too.

[13] Sources: Farr Manuscript and Fraser genealogies.

[14] Their happiness was brief, for misfortune awaited the young couple. John Mor or 'Big John of the Markets' was, like his father, a cattle-drover. Like his father too, he would follow the cause of the doomed Stuarts, and his children would later be chased from the lands of their forefathers by their cousin William of Dunmaglass.

independent nation rather than as an appendage to England; and from the laird of M'Intosh, who hated the Whig Member of Parliament, Duncan Forbes of Culloden, because his new power challenged his own ancestral authority.

Young Farquhar and his brother William were made captains in the 800-man M'Intosh Regiment, as was the not-so-young Farquhar of Dalcrombie or Aberchalder in Lonnie. M'Gillivray, M'Queen and M'Intosh cousins and their kinsmen tenants of the farms in Strathnairn swelled the numbers of the Jacobite force. First, together with their parish minister, they laid siege to Forbes' stronghold in Culloden, and then marched with M'Intosh of Borlum across the border. The expected Jacobite uprising in England did not happen and they were forced to surrender at Preston.

Among the Jacobite prisoners were many M'Gillivrays who were transported in shackles from Liverpool to South Carolina, Maryland, Jamaica and Antigua. Nothing is known about the fate of these M'Gillivrays, except for one. For those that did not die in the hold, the chances of survival were higher in America than in the West Indies, where harsh working conditions and tropical disease took a heavy toll. One of the Lauchlans transported on the Wakefield to America not only survived but prospered, and twenty years later, as we have seen, left a will and property. This lad was a nephew of John of Dalcrombie, and he and perhaps uncle and cousins may have been responsible for the subsequent involvement of M'Gillivrays with the New World.

The officers taken prisoner were marched into London in a mock triumphal procession followed by a jeering mob. M'Intosh of Borlum lay in prison for five months, until he and fifteen others overpowered the sentinels and escaped the night before they were to be sentenced. Young Farquhar and his brother, the Captain Ban, were among those imprisoned in London, the former named in the Bill of High Treason. James Dunbar, colonel of the Inverness militia, enemy of the Jacobites but close friend of Dunmaglass, wrote to Duncan Forbes of Culloden in March 1716 pleading for a remission for Angus M'Bean, Kynchyle's son, for he 'gave intelligence of the enemy's motion to have the rebellion subdued'. He sought similar pardons for Dunmaglass and Robert Shaw of Tordarroch. Dunmaglass was, according to Simon Fraser

Mackintosh of Farr, dismissed because there was some 'error in the indictment about his name and designation'.[15] But he added a faint perpendicular inscription: "Turned King's Evidence". So it was believed that Farquhar had been a traitor to the Jacobite forces, like M'Bean.

On 3 June 1716, a week before the trial, Farquhar's brother, the Captain Ban, escaped from Newgate prison, together with James M'Queen and his father-in-law Angus M'Intosh of Kyllachy, wrapped in women's clothing. They probably all owed their lives to their superior Sir Hugh Campbell who interceded for his M'Intosh relation, although the Earl of Moray may also have played a part.

Whether Farquhar turned King's evidence or not, he returned to Inverness, lucky to be alive. The minister Michael Fraser stood trial, accused of open disloyalty and of neglecting to pray for the new Protestant sovereign and the royal family as required by law, and of avowing his enmity to the constitution. Fraser promised to resign but was in fact left in his parish unmolested.

If Dunmaglass was lucky, his property was less fortunate: his home at Gask was plundered, papers and movables gone. He took up his former life as farmer and excelled at business, but 'interfering too much with other people's affairs, his own became involved', according to Fraser-Mackintosh. Bailie John Steuart, on the other hand, who quipped he was 'the son of a very honest woman', described him as a 'sensible' man. In 1717 he married his cousin Elizabeth M'Intosh of Aberarder. They had a son, Alexander, then three daughters; a second son, William, was not born until 1732. According to Farr, a string of others came late in the marriage; there is no record of their early existence in Scotland.

William, the Captain Ban, had married Janet M'Intosh of Kyllachy the year before the rebellion. The couple may have initially settled in Petty, although in March 1717 Bailie John Steuart protested against his instructions from the Earl of Moray to make room for William: 'I think it will be a hardship to remove such honest tennents on so short advertisement....I must say I am already sick of too many gentlemen tennents in Pettie.' By 1727 William and his family were at the farm at Gask, perhaps sharing with

---

[15] Source cited: Secret History of the Rebellion, Newgate 1715

William's brother. The former Jacobite officer and gentleman farmer was now a cattle drover, taking the Gask or Dunmaglass herds to market. The main market of the year was the great tryst at Crieff; it turned the drovers into the financiers of the Highlands, as accounts were settled and solvency once again obtained. Like his fellow lairds and tacksmen, the Captain Ban would cut a fine figure as he rode through mountain and glen with a poignard at his belt, a knife and fork in a sheath, a pistol, a snuff mull in front and a great broadsword at his side, for drovers were exempt from the Disarming Acts. In his pockets undoubtedly there were bills to exchange or collect; Alexander in Lonnie would have accompanied him south, charged with Bailie John Steuart's business deals.

William died in 1734, perhaps as a result of a beating from persons unknown who ambushed him near Loch Duntelchaig. The Captain Ban attained immortality in the Highlands as the intrepid hero of a story involving candles, fairies and a damsel in distress recounted, inter alia, by David Thomson in *Nairn in Darkness or Light*.[16]

Diverse legal summons sent to his grieving widow and children, to settle his debts to the Dalcrombie family at Lonnie (recently indexed in the Inverness archives) show that his children were named Lachlan, Alexander, Charles, William, Farquhar, Louisa and Emilia.[17] In addition, he had an early natural son, John (John 'Mor' or 'Big John of the Markets' in Gask) who would die heroically at Culloden, leaving a young family that his wife, the daughter of the Jacobite minister we have just referred to, struggled to bring up.[18]

Of Farquhar and the Captain Ban's two brothers, Donald and David, little is known, other than that Donald was a sheriff-officer in Inverness and David married a distant M'Gillivray cousin at Mid-

---

[16] In David Thomson's account, the hero is Dunmaglass (recently returned from Africa) and not his brother; the woman he rescues is the wife of the M'Intosh laird. Simon Fraser Mackintosh's shorter version is given in the Appendix.

[17] Summons of Cognition, Execution M'Gillivray against MacIntosh &c, 1734, Inverness archives. Emilia is also the name of William's mother.

[18] The names of these M'Gillivray children are not known. SC29/10/420, National Archives of Scotland, Edinburgh

Leys.[19] The latter's only known child was Alexander, born in 1727. This ancestry is easy to prove as Alexander's baptism is registered in the parish records, unlike the others who appear in this history. Alexander had two sons and four daughters. One son was an armourer and last known to be living in Liverpool, the other died childless. The four daughters married local farmers named Fraser, Fraser, Rose and Paterson, and their descendants who represented their families in the competition for the non-entailed lands were variously a medical student in Canada (also descended from McTavish of Dunardry), a salmon-fisher in Caithness, a Strathnairn farmer and a merchant in the north of England.[20] Again, it would be the descendants of the next eldest brother of Farquhar of Dunmaglass who would be the heirs-at-law. So the issue was: who was the next eldest brother of Farquhar, and who were his descendants?

Who is Jean ?

Tradition relates that the Captain Ban's sixteen-year-old son Lachlan crossed the seas to Charles Town, ending up in 1740 with the coveted Indian trader's licence that had previously belonged to Archibald M'Gillivray. From then on Lachlan acquired much power and prestige, and amassed great wealth. Simon Fraser Mackintosh of Farr - Inverness lawyer and genealogist, the first historian sui generis of the M'Gillivray family, who had a M'Gillivray mother - was the source of information regarding Lachlan's parentage.[21] At any rate, when Lachlan returned as a rich man from America towards the end of his life, it was to settle at Dunmaglass and bring up his orphaned infant relation, John Lachlan, who was titular chief of the clan, and apparently claim a sister named Jean. Farr mentions only three siblings for Lachlan: William, Jean and Lucy. The 1734

---

[19] The Inverness deaths register for 1747 mentions the death of a child Janet, daughter of Donald M'Gillivray of Dunmaglass. We don't know this Donald's position in the genealogies.

[20] Descendants of the Strathnairn family are still present today in the area; sadly nothing has come down to them about the litigation.

[21] There was undoubtedly much business for lawyers specializing in genealogy at a time when many who made their wealth in the colonies died with closest relatives in Scotland.

legal summons had not mentioned any Jean. For this reason, we shall look at references to Jean with some suspicion.

Who was Jean? This question is central in determining whether there was deception or not at the inheritance litigation. Jean's grandchildren claimed their ancestor had no sister by the name of Lucy. The name of this daughter of the Captain Ban's was first rendered as Louisa, then Lucia on her marriage registration, while descendants called her Lucy. We should point out that if the Dunmaglass line failed, it would be the Captain Ban's children who would inherit Dunmaglass - the descendants of Lachlan, Alexander or the other brothers - and the non-entailed lands could go to the descendants of either or both the sisters if none of the brothers had issue. According to the genealogies that Mackintosh of Farr drew up, in the event that all these lines should fail, the inheritance would come to his own branch, the descendants of the Dalcrombies at Dalzeil.

Simon would have known the identity and ancestry of this Jean. There is much evidence that she existed: a letter that Lachlan is supposed to have written to her, as well as a mention in a typescript copy of Lachlan's 1767 will (which may not be authentic for the original remains unaccounted for).[22] Her son Lachlan is mentioned in Colonel John's 1787 will. Most importantly, Jean is given as the next of kin in an index of legal papers relating to the child John Lachlan. She was married firstly to a Duncan Roy M'Gillivray of the farm Balnagaig on the Dunmaglass estate, and secondly to a John Mor M'Gillivray, who took his place on the farm. Her existence seems so substantive and her sisterhood to Lachlan so undisputed that we might be tempted to conclude that the names of William's children were given incorrectly in the various legal summons, were it not for numerous inconsistencies in this history that strengthen doubts that she was in fact the daughter of the Captain Ban. If she was indeed Lachlan's sister, we would suspect that Lachlan's parentage has also been wrongly reported.

Almost a hundred and fifty years after the birth of the Captain Ban's children, various descendants of either Lucy or Jean were competing with each other in collecting evidence to support their

---

[22] This typescript will is often used as a primary document.

claims that they were the lawful heirs. Were Simon Fraser Mackintosh's genealogies used as a source or were they drawn up subsequently? Had he shuffled the cards prior to litigation or laid them out after the game was over?

Another genealogy tree, not as detailed or annotated as Farr's, predates the litigation by several years. It was drawn up by Reverend Duncan Mackenzie with the help of his M'Gillivray mother-in-law, a sister of Simon Mackintosh of Farr's mother. McKenzie was the Episcopal minister in Strathnairn and John Lachlan's close friend and spiritual guide. The salient point is that his genealogies include neither the Captain Ban, nor his attributed children Lachlan and Jean. While Mackintosh of Farr's genealogies show the Canadian branch to be loose, appearing out of nowhere and unrelated to the Dunmaglasses, Rev. Mackenzie makes no mention at all of the Captain Ban's branch, the principal heirs to Dunmaglass.[23]

Central in both genealogies is the much stronger and successful branch descending through a Dalcrombie of Dalzeil, next to which the other branches seem to have withered and died, or have been pruned away. Had John Lachlan simply never mentioned his childhood or his great benefactor Lachlan to his friend Rev. Mackenzie? The fact that he might not have is meaningful – but what does it mean?

The new Dunmaglass

Let us return to the Dunmaglass family and its different identifiable members. Farquhar, the head, died about 1740 and was succeeded by his son Alexander. This Alexander would become the best known of the M'Gillivray chiefs on account of his bravery at the Battle of Culloden when he led the M'Intosh forces. According to clan history, he was pressed into service by two fair ladies, Anne Farquharson, the wife of the laird of M'Intosh and his betrothed Elizabeth, daughter of Duncan Campbell, a 1715 Jacobite in exile in Rome, of the family of Clunas and Cawdor. He died a hero at

---

[23] His genealogies are given in the Appendix

Culloden, but his family suffered as a result. Alexander's inclusion in the Act of Attainder meant the forfeiture of his lands, but this was somehow reversed by their lawyer cousin, William M'Intosh of Holm.[24]

We can put together the history of the Dunmaglass family in the years that followed thanks to Charles Fraser-Mackintosh, MP and Highland historian, and his written account of the clan.

Alexander was succeeded by his much younger brother William who was born in 1732 and attended Mr. Raining's Free Charity School at Inverness. In 1759, like other young Highlanders who joined the army for no better future awaited them in their homelands, William bought a commission and raised his own company. By this time, recruits were scarce so he resorted to means of coercion similar to those used by the infamous John Macpherson in Ballachroan: getting men drunk, putting the King's shilling in their pockets and the next day calling his due.[25] In mid-December one Donald Fraser, farmer, accused him of forced enlistment. Fraser said he had been given dram after dram at Mr. Clarke's at Milburn until he could no longer understand what he was doing, that he had a motherless child and was willing to return the levy money. In contrast, Simon Fraser Mackintosh wrote that Dunmaglass was so popular that there were no fewer than 15 John M'Gillivrays recruited.

Before leaving, William put his affairs in order. He gave up the overdue testament dative of his brother Alexander, and appointed a commission to look after his property during his absence. This comprised the Hon. Aeneas M'Intosh of M'Intosh, Mr. Shaw, a merchant in Inverness, Farquhar M'Gillivray of Dalcrombie, his old tutor and cousin William M'Intosh of Holm, and his sister-german Anne. His mother and sisters may have moved as Dunmaglass was leased to the dwarf Alexander Fraser, the second son of Lord Lovat, until his death in 1762.

---

[24] Son of Anna M'Gillivray of Dunmaglass and John M'Intosh of Holm

[25] The Macphails of Inverairnie in *Minor Septs of Clan Chattan* by Charles Fraser-Mackintosh. He was one of the two most wicked men in Inverness in the 18th century, the other being Farquhar M'Gillivray of Dalcrombie. Ballachroan's infamy and power over the people of Badenoch have been widely described, by Sir Walter Scott and more recently by Meta Scarlett in In the Glens where I was young.

While Captain William and his company served in the East Indies for four years, his younger brothers John, Donald and Farquhar were reportedly already in America. Their wealthy relation Lachlan had said he would make John his heir, a promise he was later to duplicate to his brother William. John set up as a trader in Florida, buying deerskins from the Indians in exchange for trinkets imported from England. In little time he amassed a fortune comparable to Lachlan's. He would later be known as Colonel John when he raised a company of some hundred soldiers to defend the Mississippi frontier. Brother Farquhar is variously said to have been a carpenter, a church minister and a tutor of Latin to Lachlan's celebrated Creek son Alexander M'Gillivray, and Donald was a sea captain in command of a vessel owned by Lachlan, or working for John in Florida.

Lachlan and his sister Jean

As we have mentioned, Lachlan had come to America in 1737, when he was very young, with plenty of determination and a network of family relations headed by the successful Archibald, who would soon return to Scotland. Lachlan progressed from trader to planter, and advised the authorities on policy concerning the Indians. His commercial success and position brought him wealth and extensive lands. After many years spent at Little Tallassee in the Creek country where he had at least three children, including the celebrated Alexander, chief of the Creek Nation, he ended up living at his Vale Royal estate in Savannah. His total holdings exceeded 10,000 acres, making him one of the largest landowners in the province. His experience of Indian life, customs and language, and his moderation, skill and diplomacy placed him in a privileged position with both the Creeks and the British.

An Alexander, a sea mariner born in 1720 living in Charles Town, is reported to be Lachlan's brother.[26] Alexander died in

---

[26] This Alexander was married to Elizabeth Patchable (sic), perhaps a daughter of Theodore Pachelbel (son of Johann the musician), who at this time lived in Charleston, where he was a musical instrument maker and organist. Alexander was claimed as ancestor by Hugh Swinton M'Gillivray of America, through an attributed son William. These M'Gillivrays are mentioned in the 1757 will of Lachlan's fellow trader, Donald

1763; his will mentions his wife Elizabeth and his brother Lachlan. The following year, Lachlan made a quick voyage to England to establish new trade connections. A Charles Town merchant wrote to a correspondent that M'Gillivray was taking passage for London and would visit him; he described him as 'an honest man' and 'a generous merchant'. Lachlan sailed in May and was back in Savannah by September. Did he meet William, recently back from the East Indies, in London? If so, what did they say to one another? Lachlan was now determined to return home and put a series of notices in *The Georgia Gazette* that he would be leaving for England the following spring; he called upon all those indebted to him to pay what they owed to avoid being sued. Archibald's eldest son, John, scarcely into his teens, seems to have joined him in Georgia about this time, and perhaps just as Archibald had handed over to Lachlan to return to the homeland, Lachlan planned to leave things in the hands of Archibald's son in turn. It is pleasing to think that Archibald, in the Highlands of Scotland, might have taught his young sons not Latin and Greek but the Creek language to prepare them for their future. But there is no mention of John again after 1767 and, according to Farr, he died in Carolina. In the end, Lachlan did not leave.

On 12 June 1767, Lachlan supposedly wrote a will, which exists only in printed form among the 19th century litigation papers at Inverness Library. The whereabouts of the original hand-written will, if there was one, are not known. In this will is the earliest mention of Lachlan's sister Jean.

Lachlan made his main bequests to his Scottish family: he left Vale Royal and Hutchinson's Island, together with all his possessions and slaves, to his cousin John, the son of Farquhar M'Gillivray of Dunmaglass, Esquire, merchant at Mobile in West

---

Clark, in Charles Town, probably of the Clarks who shared the M'Gillivray farm of Dalzeil, for Donald refers to his brother, Alexander in Petty, near Castle Steuart. Among his legatees are Laughlan M'Gillivray, Alexander M'Gillivray and wife, and John M'Gilvray; his books were bequeathed to William M'Gillivray and William Sluthers. Laughlan was one of his executors, and the will was witnessed by Hanna Patchable. That Lachlan, Indian trader, had a brother in Charlestown in 1758 is confirmed by a letter written by Atkin: 'Mr. M'Gillivray having given me notice of a Resolution he hath taken suddenly (at least as far as I know) to go to Charlestown tomorrow morning. On account of the Danger his Brother is supposed to be in his life…'

Florida. If John were to die without lawful sons, then the estates would go to John's eldest brother William of Dunmaglass, and if William were also to die without heirs, co-heirs would be the eldest sons of Archibald M'Gillivray of Daviot and Farquhar M'Gillivray of Dalcrombie (no relationship specified).

He bequeathed one thousand pounds to his natural son Alexander, born in 1750, then apprenticed to Messrs Inglis and Hall, merchants in Savannah. If Alexander were to die without sons, this legacy would go to Lachlan's sister Jean M'Gillivray in Inverness and to his cousin Farquhar M'Gillivray (John's brother at Mobile, West Florida).

There were further bequests to his cousins James M'Intosh in West Florida and Alexander M'Intosh, merchant in Mobile and the Indian countries, £500 to Lachlan, son of Archibald M'Gillivray of Daviot, £500 to Daniel M'Gillivray of James Jackson and Co. in Augusta (no relationship specified); if Daniel were to die before he did, then the money would go to the second living son of his sister Jean.[27] Non-family beneficiaries included friends and business partners.

The residue of his estate would be divided among five sets of heirs, his son Alexander, his cousin John, the children of his sister Jean, his cousin William and his merchant friends John Graham and Alexander Inglis.

If Lachlan was son of the Captain Ban, the Alexander M'Intosh referred to in the will could have been the son of Anna of Dunmaglass and John M'Intosh of Holm; this John had earlier gone to Darien, and then returned to Scotland where he died. In 1767, there was an Alexander M'Intosh in Mobile who was an Indian trader and elected member of the West Florida Commons House of Assembly, who we presume from this will was Holm's son, born in Scotland in 1718. The cousin James M'Intosh of Kyllachy was a fellow Indian trader in Florida, whose sister Archibald M'Gillivray had married on his return to Scotland. There was some rift between James and Archibald or his children, for in James' will – he died in 1787 - he 'for ever' excluded any of these children from claiming

---

[27] This Daniel may be Donald M'Gillivray of Dunmaglass who was reportedly a sea-captain.

his estate. He would have known John, James and Lachlan. Some of his lands on the Tombigbee bordered on one of Colonel John's tracts of land, the Sunflowers.

There is no doubt that Lachlan was a generous man. Given the extent of the bequests, the omissions appear incongruous. There is no mention of any of his brothers or sisters in America or Scotland, except for a Jean; we know that the Captain Ban's daughter Lucy had at least one child in Nairn, and there is some indication that her brother William was alive. Lachlan fails to mention a widowed sister-in-law (the wife of his brother Alexander who had died a few years previously), and perhaps a nephew in America, but includes more distant relatives in Scotland that he may not have known. Relations with the Dalcrombies had been far from close. First, Farquhar of Dalcrombie's father had taken legal action against Lachlan's widowed mother a year or two before Lachlan left Scotland, and then Farquhar himself instigated legal proceedings against Lachlan for the settlement of his father's debt.

In the absence of a handwritten original, it is tempting to conclude that the will is not authentic. The legatees in America are plausible but those in Scotland are unorthodox although they conform to the genealogies drawn up later by lawyer Simon Fraser Mackintosh, who also omitted any mention of Lachlan's brother Alexander. We know from historical documents that Lachlan did have a brother in America; and he was most likely named Alexander. Bailie John Steuart wrote in 1749 that he had in his hands a letter from 'Mrs. Mackgilvrays, William McGilvrays widow', to her son Alexander in Carolina. In addition both Alexander and Lachlan appear as beneficiaries in the will of Lachlan's fellow-trader Daniel Clark who had come to Charleston from Dalzeil. Another beneficiary in Clark's will was a William M'Gillivray, who remains unidentified but could have been Alexander's infant son, as claimed by a M'Gillivray family in America.

Certain details in the will could only be known to those with an intimate knowledge of Lachlan: the name of his godson, James Barnard, or an appropriate date for the birth of his son Alexander, unknown to American historians until the discovery of the printed will in Inverness. This copy could therefore be a revised version of an original document.

If Lachlan was son of another M'Gillivray and not the Captain Ban, he too would doubtlessly have M'Intosh cousins: the two families were so intrinsically intermarried that different branches might share the same cousins. If we attempt to follow one thread, it soon disappears into the thick sturdy fabric of generations of M'Intoshes who, like property-owning families in poor societies throughout the world, intermarried to ensure retention of their land.[28]

Alternatively, the will could be authentic but this Lachlan is not the son of the Captain Ban. The question then would be not why William of Dunmaglass recognized Lachlan as his cousin - he could have been a more remote relation - but why he is placed in this position in the genealogies. If the will is a fake concocted at a later date or is a modified version of an authentic document to claim relationships for the inheritance, we are in an unenviable position.

---

[28] Lachlan had M'Intosh of Holm cousins on his father's side, and M'Intosh of Kyllachy on his mother's. Janet was one of a dozen children, so Lachlan may have had several dozen cousins, many with the same first name, including the children of i) Christian who married John M'Intosh, merchant (sons included John, Provost of Inverness and Charles, Colonel John's lawyer), ii) Katherine who married M'Intosh of Corrybrough in Auchindown, Cawdor (the latter had four sons who died in Jamaica or the Bahamas, including a James). Anne Fraser of Balnain was also a cousin, with a Kyllachy mother.

If Lachlan was a brother of Archibald and Alexander, with a M'Intosh of Daviot mother who was one of twelve or more children, he would have had countless Daviot cousins. Dr. Anthony W. Parker in *Scottish Highlanders in Colonial Georgia* identifies a John M'Intosh, brother to the chief, in Georgia in 1740. In addition, Lachlan would have had cousins through aunts named Johnston, Fraser of Dunchea, M'Pherson of Strathmachie, McAulay and Mackenzie.

If Lachlan had neither of these mothers, there are other M'Intosh lads who could 'fit' here. Cousins in America could have been i) sons of Duncan of Castleleathers (and uncles or brothers of the Laird of M'Intosh), ii) James of Abererder (first cousin of Dunmaglass) who died in America in 1769 iii) James, merchant in New York and son of William Roy in Termit iv) Captain Alexander of Culclachy (first cousin of Dunmaglass) who died in America in 1776 v) Alexander, brother of John Mor M'Intosh, who, according to one source at the litigation, was illegitimate; he died circa 1779 at about the same time as Alexander of Holm vi) sons of Lt M'Intosh of Mid-Coul of whom there was at least one – James - in Savannah.

An early Margaret M'Gillivray married John M'Intosh, a settler in Darien, of the Borlum family, before 1745. She seems to have been in America before her marriage and would have been daughter of one of the M'Gillivray families in this history.

What do we retain as authentic to understand the relationships of the Dunmaglass M'Gillivrays?

We should here mention a second will, Colonel John's, drawn up that same year, also only in printed form. His bequests are mainly to his immediate family, as well as to Lachlan. His brother William was his principal heir. Then to Lachlan, his cousin, he gave £1000 and his Negro Paul. Farquhar, his brother and business partner in Mobile, was bequeathed £250 and his brother Donald or Daniel £400. Sisters Betsy and Catherine would get £100 each, and sister Anne £200. Smaller legacies went to John, son of Archibald of Daviot, then in Georgia (this is the only mention of this John); his old wet nurse in Inverness and her son then in Mobile; and Finlay M'Gillivray, overseer at Lachlan's plantation. His livestock was left to his two 'reputed sons Samuel and William begotten upon two Indian women in the Chickesaw country'. Generous legacies went to business relations of his company, M'Gillivray and Swanson, leading traders and shippers in Florida. Colonel John's experience and skill had put him, like Lachlan, in a position to give advice in the continually changing policies of the authorities: warmongering, peacekeeping or non-intervention, and he too had amassed considerable wealth.

William's letter

If Lachlan hadn't seen William of Dunmaglass in London in 1764 or if William hadn't visited America, Lachlan would remember him as a four year-old. It would appear that the two men corresponded, discussing family matters and William's personal aspirations. The printed litigation documents include a letter dated 23 August 1769 that is 'supposed to be written to Lachlan (commonly called Lea)'. We take this to mean that there was not the customary addressee for the scribe to refer to, which in our opinion discredits the authenticity. The thick paper used for 18th century correspondence was folded, refolded and sealed, with the addressee written directly on the verso. This letter carries the second mention of Jean, sister to Lachlan. However untrustworthy the contents of this letter may be, we learn that William had recently bought her a farm, that she had a number of children, the two eldest being of school age, that Lachlan was pressing William to marry and continue his line, and William's answer as to why he had chosen not to do so. He also suggested he would not look unkindly on another branch of the family inheriting Dunmaglass.

Dear Cousin, My brother Donald spent a part of the summer with me here, and seems to be kind, honest, and blunt, like the generality of his profession. He made very affectionate mention of you, and said you was extremely kind and obliging to him, and promised to join John in buying a vessel for him. He was in hopes of sailing outwards in the vessel which Captain Minns has at present, but the Captain begged to be allowed this voyage in order to settle his affairs, which was complied with, so that Donald goes as mate.

He flattered me with the hopes of seeing you in Britain last summer; I own my expectations were almost extinguished, but his assuring me that you had disengaged yourself from trade, and was, about the time he left you, even talking of putting aboard your sea-stock, raised my hopes; but they are again fallen into their former state of suspense and doubt. In one of your letters, you wanted me to marry, to which paragraph I omitted hitherto making any answer, but as silence on that head, or any other wherein you want satisfaction, might justly deserve your blame, and as I think friendship and our connection should banish all reserve, and produce a free and easy communication of thought, I will state that matter as it really is. The family estate is but small; it devolved on me deeply burdened, in which situation it still remains. I have my mother and my sisters to support, and to say the truth, my own turn of mind above my income; were matrimony to be added to this amount, what would be the consequence? What judgment would the world pass, and, what is still more severe, what would be my own?

I own the prospect does not appear inviting to me, who am not strong enough to imagine myself superior to the frown and slings of fortune; nor can any degree of observation justify my presuming, that any of the fair sex that I might

41

involve in my circumstances would prove so, even supposing I had philosophy enough for it myself. But may I not with more justice ask, why you do not alter your condition, as your own industry, good fortune and conduct have removed the impediments that stand in my way, and as it is extremely just and natural that your children should enjoy the labour and fatigue of a number of years spent in a disagreeable climate, and frequently exposed to dangers? Your constitution is, according to my information, pretty good, therefore all the remaining arguments are of little force, unless you are averse to that state of life, and can hardly satisfy either your friends or yourself.

Neither can I see why my brother John should not marry, as he is advancing towards an independency. And I can assure you, with the utmost regard to truth, that am equally well satisfied that his issue, or yours should represent the family of Dunmaglass as my own, so far as I can judge at present of my own heart. The qualities of John's heart are very high, in my esteem. Farquhar is, it seems, married, but what sort of gentleman he is, I know not, but he has discontinued, without any cause on my part that I am acquainted with, writing me, or, indeed any of his relations in this part of the world, notwithstanding my frequently soliciting him on that head.

Sanders, your uncle David's son, is one of those characters that have very little either of good or ill in them. He made a mean marriage, nor could I discover in any of the instances wherein I had occasion to try him, that his spirit could rise much beyond that level. He has a throng (sic) family, but too poor to afford them education. But am afraid I have transgressed on your patience on this subject.

I have given a farm of £6 to your sister Jean and her husband, and if I find that more will be of advantage to them they will have it, bought what cattle, with what they had themselves was thought a sufficient stocking, till their farm was brought to better order and conveniency of houses, &c; paid all their debts, and put their two eldest boys to school in the country – all which amounts to £55 sterling. The balance

I have in my hands, and will be laid out as much to their advantage as I can. The plan I laid down for her and family is this, that their farm should be rent free, that the fees of a man and maid servant to assist them in the management of it should be likewise paid, and their children, as they came of proper age, sent to school. For a year or two, they may want a little farther assistance, such as a little meal, which I will give them in, but when these matters are brought to a proper method and order, should they manage but tolerably well, I think it may become unnecessary. This plan, so far as it is extended at present, will amount yearly to between £16 and £17 sterling, without taking meal or any such little necessary into accompt – viz. to rent £6; to board for the two boys, and a schoolmaster's dues, £7.6s; to a fee and shoes, &c, to a man-servant, £2.6s; to ditto for a maid-servant £1.4s. On the whole, I suppose it may cost you £20 yearly till more of the children are fit for school. Your sister sends you a thousand thanks and blessings, which she desires me deliver in her name.

My brother Donald told me you wanted somebody from this country to oversee a plantation. There is the youngest son of William M'Gillivray, tenant in Balnagaik of Dunmaglass – he was better known by the name of William – a man who is very desirous of going, but as he is married, would know what encouragement he was to expect, or how much, he would depend on yearly. He is honest, can write, read and has learned the common rules of arithmetic.

One Mrs. Lessly, a parson's widow here, has opportuned me to write you, in order to learn what effects of money a natural brother of her's that died, t'other year, at a gentleman's house near Savannah, was worth at his death, and how it is disposed of. She is daughter to one Lachlane More M'Intosh, uncle to this present Borlum; her father lived at Knocknagael for sometime, and died afterwards in the place of Borlum. There are brother's children of the man that died lately in that country, but she would not be satisfied without my writing you. Finlay M'Gillivray, of whose death you wrote me, was the person who wrote to this country in order to learn who were next heirs to this man M'Intosh, and procure a power of attorney to remit them home the money as he gave out. They will be uneasy till your answer comes. Will you tell me what kind of woman Farquhar's wife is, if they have children, and what they are doing? Were she agreeable to John, I hardly think he would have observed silence for so long on that head.

I am, Will. M'Gillivray

The letter states that Jean received a farm in 1769 – we learn from a later note that this is Balnagaig. Her descendants would claim at the litigation that she had been in Balnagaig before 1757 by which time her eldest daughter was born, and remained there until at least 1803. Legal papers confirm the presence of a Duncan and his brother Donald in Balnagaig in 1762; their father, William, was principal tenant as early as 1746. Lachlan would have known this farm - his sister was apparently married to William in Balnagaig's son or brother - so it is odd that its tenants should need describing. It is also curious that Finlay M'Gillivray should have been looking to Scotland for relations of the deceased M'Intosh when there were more than enough heirs in Georgia of this man's brother, John Mohr M'Intosh, leader of Darien.

Captain William in America

In 1770, Lachlan returned to Inverness for an extended visit. A business acquaintance of the time wrote that Lachlan's mother had died a few weeks prior to his arrival. In *The McGillivray and McIntosh Traders on the Old Southwest Frontier 1716-1815*, Amos Wright holds that the Captain Ban's wife, Janet M'Intosh, had died by 1743 when the Dunmaglass heirs were trying to recover sums granted her on her marriage to the Captain Ban, a procedure engaged only after the death of a party to the marriage. If this is the case, it would be incontrovertible proof that Lachlan was not the son of the Captain Ban and Janet M'Intosh.

During the two years or so that Lachlan was in Scotland, Captain William, who had sold his commission in the army six years before and would complain bitterly of his poverty, was able to buy several properties that were clearly financed by Lachlan: Faillie, Glenmazeran and Inverernie.[29] These purchases had been preceded by a one-off valuation in February 1770 of the teinds of William's lands of Dunmaglass, Lairgs and Gask. In addition, or in unregistered exchange for land he held in Scotland, Lachlan made over to William a rice plantation in Hutchison's Island, off Charleston. In October 1772, Lachlan returned to America; with him went William.[30]

Not long after taking possession of his rice plantation and slaves at Gask on Hutchinson Island, William of Dunmaglass was off travelling. In the summer of 1773 he and two unnamed brothers (perhaps Colonel John and Donald, the sea captain, or Farquhar), went for a 'tour of pleasure' to the Mohawk lands in upstate New York, where they visited Sir William Johnson, the Indian Superintendent of the Northern Department, as well as Master of the Albany Lodge of Free Masons and Provincial Grand Master of New York. The former master of the Scottish lodge, St. Andrew's Kilwinning, carried a letter of introduction. He needed no introduction, however, to old friends already living on Sir William's estate.

Many years earlier, two of the regimental captains in the Fraser's Highlanders in the Seven Years' War were John McTavish of Garthbeg and Hugh Fraser. One of McTavish's daughters was married to Donald Roy M'Gillivray[31], born at Balnagaig farm, one of his sons was married to Anne, daughter of Alexander M'Gillivray of the Carolinas and Knocknagael. Back in Scotland, Hugh Fraser married another of McTavish's daughters. Together with her

---

[29] In May 1771, William borrowed £700 from M'Intosh of Culclachy, with payment terms of an unheard-of 20% interest by Martinmas; loans always carried a standard 5% p.a. interest. Glenmazeran passed on to M'Intosh of Aberarder.

[30] There is no trace of William for four years before he moved to America. In 1768 he sold the lands of Bochrubin to Fraser of Balnain and was able to settle debts towards the M'Intosh of Aberarder children to whom he was curator. He also accepted a one-year appointment as Master of the St Andrew's Kilwinning Lodge in Inverness; his father and Donald of Dalcrombie had both belonged to St. John's Kilwinning, supposedly the oldest lodge in Britain.

[31] The Dores marriage registration of 26 January 1764 carries the double name Roy M'Gillivray.

thirteen-year-old brother, Simon, they returned to America with a party of emigrants from Stratherrick, settling on the vast estates of Sir William Johnson, who lived in a grand colonial house and was a welcoming host. Life here was centred on the fur trade. Young Simon McTavish lived at Johnson Hall for two years until he found work with Commodore Alexander Grant of Glenmoriston, in charge of the British naval vessels on the Great Lakes. After entering the fur trade as an outfitter, he founded the North West Company, eventually entrusting the running of the company to his nephew William M'Gillivray, son of Donald Roy and his sister Ann.

Fraser seems to have engaged in unsuccessful land speculation in the Mohawk Valley and New Hampshire. It was during this period that Dunmaglass and his two brothers visited the Scottish settlement. Perhaps they were looking for a good investment. Settlement was now spreading into the Ohio country even though no peace treaty had been concluded with the Indians. There is a tale among the Creeks that Lachlan intended to move his activities and family up north. Whatever their intention, there is something enigmatic about three middle-aged M'Gillivray brothers, whose identities are not clear, one perhaps a sea-captain, another an Indian trader and the last fresh from Scotland, making their way by boat, horse or wagon from Albany to Schenectady, and from there to the outpost in Indian country where their McTavish connections lived.

Early the following year, 1774, an unidentified man died at Lachlan's plantation, Vale Royal. A coroner's inquest returned that the man was murdered by persons unknown. The man may have been Farquhar, reportedly murdered, but we do not know whether this Farquhar was the son of Dunmaglass or of the Captain Ban, whether he was the cabinetmaker, Presbyterian minister or another.[32]

The thrust for independence was now growing in America, and William was not to remain there for long. He returned to London within a few years, in advance of his relations who would stay on and try to save their American assets.

---

[32] Amos Wright reports that Farquhar, cabinetmaker, was dead by 18 January 1771.

CHAPTER THREE

DUNMAGLASS' RELATIONS IN SCOTLAND IN THE 18TH CENTURY

Dalzeil descendants

To identify John Lachlan's closest kin in the 19th century, it is important to describe the extended Dunmaglass family a hundred years previously, to trace affinities and establish how assets and wealth changed hands. So who were the relations of John Lachlan's father in Scotland? The battle of Culloden had taken the lives of a number of the Dalcrombie M'Gillivrays. In the Lonnie family, Farquhar survived. Robert, Archibald and Alexander all had children so a new generation had sprung from the Dalzeil M'Gillivrays.

On his return from Charles Town a month or two before the battle, Archibald married Lucy, the daughter of James M'Intosh of Kyllachy in Connage, chamberlain to the Earl of Moray; they settled at the farm of Kerrugair on the Connage estate between Inverness and Nairn.[33] Archibald farmed and traded meal for tallow, beef, bohca tea and other household necessities with his wife's relative, Bailie John M'Intosh at Inverness. Soon, however, he bought the 'wadset' or lease of Daviot from his cousin, the laird of M'Intosh, and moved from the coastal lands at Petty into Highland foothills. He had five sons, John, James, Aeneas, Alexander and Lachlan, and three daughters, Marjory, Janet and Anne. Lucy died at the birth of her youngest daughter and Archibald was left at the head of a family of eight young children. (The only mention of Aeneas, Marjory and Anne is with reference to their birth.)

Archibald may have been a 'gentleman farmer', but given his past industriousness it would be surprising if he led an inactive life. He may well have continued a packhorse messenger service as he

---

[33] At Connage vessels unloaded contraband spirits from overseas before continuing into Inverness. Bailie John Steuart organised this at least once. The traffic must have been in the hands of local families.

had business with a certain M'Bean who owned horse stables in Inverness. If so, it would appear that his business was unsuccessful; two of his children who survived to the end of the century continually complained of their poverty.

Archibald's brother Alexander, who had preceded him to Scotland, married Anne Fraser of Balnain, who had a M'Intosh of Kyllachy mother. She was a woman of uncommon powers of mind and superior cultivation. They also had a large family, with six surviving children: John, Jean, Marjory, Anne, Catharine and Mary.[34]

The family moved from Dalzeil to Knocknagael on the hills south of Inverness. Nothing is known about Alexander's life during these years. If he had previously been a financier, there are no documents that suggest he continued this. As we have already noted, he and his family may have moved back to Carolina. Thomas de Quincey wrote that their daughter Marjorie was a native of the colony. Alexander's gravestone records that he died in 1753 aged 57. His widow and children are next found at Clune, a farmhouse overlooking Loch Ness, on the Balnain estate at Auldourie belonging to Anne's brother, William Fraser of Balnain, writer to the Signet, and his wife, daughter of the Lord Provost of Edinburgh. Of the M'Gillivray families at the time, they were undoubtedly the most well-connected.

The Episcopalian Bishop Forbes, who devoted his life to bearing witness to the failed Jacobite rebellion in northern Scotland, wrote that he had tea with Anne in 1762 at the old farmhouse. Her daughters married when they came of age: Marjory to John M'Intosh of Kyllachy, the brother of Archibald's deceased wife and the son of the chamberlain to the Earl of Moray. As a captain in Keith's Highlanders (68th), M'Intosh moved with his regiment from Ireland to Antigua and Gibraltar. Marjory remained with her sisters and mother at the house at Clune, bitterly unhappy at being separated from her husband and having little money to raise her children.

---

[34] This may have been his second marriage; in 1726, a marriage between an Alexander in Dalzeil and Margaret Macpherson of Mid-Coul is recorded.

Marjory's sister Anne married twice, with issue by both McTavish husbands. The youngest sister, Catherine, married a close friend of Dunmaglass, James Mackintosh of Farr, and had a string of children, including the lawyer Simon, who would become the genealogist of the Mackintoshes and related families.

The latter tells us what happened to their brother John: in 1760, he served heir to his father, went first to Guadeloupe (where he is found in 1763), then to America where apparently he was the secretary of Governor Johnstone at Pensacola, Florida, taking over presumably from James Macpherson, the author of Ossian fame.[35] John reportedly died in America at the early age of 24, perhaps some time in the mid to late 1760s. He was in Pensacola at the same time as his relation of similar age, Colonel John. Dr. E. Cashin in *Lachlan McGillivray, Indian trader, the Shaping of the Southern Colonial Frontier* treats references to John M'Gillivray in Guadeloupe and Pensacola indiscriminately as references to Colonel John. It would seem that the latter had arrived in America by 1757, worked as a merchant in Florida and also served under the governor.

In the 1770s, a drama shattered the tranquility of Clune according to Mr. Tytler-Fraser writing in the early 20th century.[36]

'In the present smoking room of Dores Lodge (Old Clune Farm House) young Fraser of Foyers and M'Gillivray of Dalcrombie were having dinner in about 1776. At that time M'Gillivray rented Clune. A quarrel suddenly broke out between them and Dalcrombie raised a bottle and hit young Foyers on the head with it. The latter was able to escape out of the back window into the yard but expired soon afterwards. M'Gillivray was a loose character and became a bankrupt. He fled to America and was grandfather of that M'Gillivray who succeeded to the estate of Dunmaglass after much litigation (1857). He had been a smith in Canada.

---

[35] James Macpherson began by collecting fragments of Gaelic poetry in the Highlands, and published between 1760 and 1764 the famous translations of Ossian, which gave rise to one of the greatest literary controversies the world has seen, and which, whatever their authenticity, played a vital part in the origin of the great Romantic movement in literature.

[36] Private publication, Gift Donations, Inverness Archives

Clune was for a time occupied by relatives of the Balnain family and Mrs. M'Intosh of Kyllachy lived there with her son, afterwards the noted statesman, philosopher and historian, Sir James Mackintosh, who was born at Aldourie in 1765. All through his life Sir James never ceased to remember with admiration the beautiful prospects by day and in moonlight from Clune House, and he regarded the first two miles of the road beyond Dores along the Lochside as the most beautiful scene he had ever witnessed.'

Sir James Mackintosh later wrote of his childhood:

'My mother was not happy. My father, a subaltern and younger brother, found his pay not too much for his own expenses, and all the kindness of her family did not deliver her mind from the painful feelings of dependence. This perhaps contributed to the extreme affection which she felt for me…There is nothing which so much lightens the burden of receiving benefits as the pleasure of conferring them.

I alone depended upon her. She loved me with that fondness which we are naturally disposed to cherish for the companion of our poverty. The only infant in a family of several women, they rivalled each other in kindness and indulgence towards me, and I think I can at this day discover in my character many of the effects of this early education.'

James was generally considered a child prodigy; at thirteen he proclaimed himself a Whig, a political stand that would never change. He spent his holidays with his grandparents at Connage, and recollects that in 1782:

'I fell violently in love with a very beautiful girl, Miss Scott, daughter of Mr. Scott, of Inverness, about three years younger than myself. I wooed her in prose and rhyme, till she returned my passion. For three or four years this amour was the principal object of my thoughts; during one half-year almost the only occupation of my time. I became impatient for an early establishment in life, which should enable me to marry.'

But to return to the murder at his house that Sir James does not mention, there is no record of it in court registers, and although young Fraser of Foyers seems to have died about this time for a younger brother inherited, there is no reference to any foul play in Fraser history. Confusingly, the descendants of John of Dalcrombie and Dalzeil, whose property was taken over by his cousin Farquhar, were continued to be known as Dalcrombie, a title Simon Fraser Mackintosh and Duncan Mackenzie both confer on them in their genealogies. The young Dalcrombie of dissolute habits referred to above (the alleged murderer) would appear to be John, the only son of Anne Fraser M'Gillivray, who had reportedly died ten years earlier, who is also confused with Colonel John in America. The dowager Mrs. M'Intosh of Kyllachy, who held court in Canterbury, referred to them in the late 1770s as this 'unhappy family of Clune'.

Rumours, whispered facts, a lack of family papers and the shared Dalcrombie designation may have induced Mr. Fraser-Tytler to mistakenly identify the dissolute character as the grandfather of the M'Gillivray who would succeed to Dunmaglass. Yet Mr. Fraser-Tytler's testimony has some authority. He was descended from Anne's brother, William Fraser of Balnain, whose only child Anne married a historian and judge, Alexander Fraser Tytler, later Lord Woodhouselee. The son of this marriage became sheriff of Inverness-shire; their great-grandson lived in the farmhouse at Clune in the early 20th century and wrote the above account. By this time, Neil John M'Gillivray of the Canadian Upper Legislature, who succeeded to Dunmaglass, had died, and his son was no longer in Inverness. The Inverness families in the know, and particularly the Fraser-Tytlers, would have been well acquainted with his claim and descent. So Mr. Fraser-Tytler's identification of the blackguard as being grandfather of the succeeding Dunmaglass is totally baffling. According to numerous legal documents, the Canadian M'Gillivray's grandfather was Farquhar M'Gillivray of Dalcrombie.

Lonnie descendant: Farquhar of Dalcrombie, the factor

Of Farquhar of Dalcrombie, Charles Fraser-Mackintosh, the 19th century Highland historian and Member of Parliament, observed: 'There were towards the end of the 18th century no two more determined and unscrupulous men in the County of Inverness than John Macpherson in Ballachroan and Farquhar M'Gillivray of Dalcrombie.'

Macpherson's reputation stems from the fear he inspired among the people of Badenoch for using devious ploys to recruit for the army. Hence the legend that he was in league with the devil. There are many anecdotes to illustrate the allegation, overshadowing the virtues accorded him by a handful of defenders who claimed that he was a land-improver ahead of his time, a kindly employer to his servants, and a friend esteemed by his equals.

There were several reports of Dalcrombie's death, but he did in fact survive until the turn of the 19th century. A paper trail in the various courts of Inverness attests to this fact although, according to some historians, inter alia John Prebble in Culloden, Dalcrombie was killed in 1746 at the age of 19 along with all his Dalcrombie kin.

Simon Fraser Mackintosh writes that this Farquhar of Dalcrombie fought at Culloden, and the official Muster Roll gives him the rank of major. As the most senior of the officers to escape unhurt, he is reported to have 'led the tattered remains of the M'Intosh Regiment from the battle-field'. All this is doubtful. There was later litigation in which Farquhar was recognised as having entered into possession of his father's farm in 1746 and had agreed that year to settle the grassum, a payment required by the landowner. He would not have remained so visible had he been an officer walking off the fields of Culloden, for retribution would have been severe. There is much information about Farquhar in the different court-records of Inverness. Like his father, who had taken Lachlan's widowed mother to court, he was of a litigious nature and engaged in over twenty court-cases.

In 1750 the Earl of Moray gave Farquhar a tack for Lonnie on condition that he fenced the fields for cattle and planted eight trees a year. Farquhar had left Lonnie by then, subletting it to Andrew Tolmie, merchant in Inverness, who in turn sublet it to Robert Macpherson of the Killihuntly family. Neither tenant nor sub-tenant ever paid and Farquhar sued. This led to a debate in the Court of Session as to whether a tenant, having only a tacit reconduction rather than a written tack, was entitled to sublet in the first instance.

Meanwhile, Farquhar lived on the wooded lands of Dalcrombie at Letterchullin on the banks of Loch Duntelchaig. In the spring of 1750, he married Miss Catharine Fraser of Farraline, whose brother Thomas appears to have married Farquhar's aunt three years earlier. Their father had married, it is said, Magdalene M'Gillivray, the sister of Dunmaglass. These continuous intermarriages, generation after generation, result in complicated family relationships, some of which had been held to be incest by the puritanical kirk in the previous century.

In 1751, the burgh of Inverness demanded repayment of a sum that had been lent just before the first rebellion to Farquhar's grandfather, Farquhar of Aberchalder, Fraser of Bochrubin and William, the Captain Ban, with guarantors Fraser of Balnain and Dunmaglass, a loan not mentioned in William's testament dative in 1734. After a forty-year moratorium, the burgh announced to Farquhar that if the loan was not paid back by the end of the week they would pursue Fraser of Balnain 'which will be disagreeable to him, as his father was no more than cautioner'. Farquhar paid, taking legal proceedings to obtain half the sum from the Captain Ban's heir – Lachlan in Charles Town.

He did this through the cautioner's son Fraser of Balnain, the brother of Anne at Clune, who was writer to the Signet in Edinburgh. Farquhar added other dues: two bonds that their fathers had given twenty years previously for black cattle purchased from the Earl of Moray's factor. Farquhar held that William had never paid his part; that he had claimed this money countless times from his eldest son Lachlan, merchant in Charles Town, but that Lachlan refused to pay the money or serve himself heir to his father as required by law. Fraser of Balnain issued a summons read at the Market Cross of Edinburgh Pier and the shore of Leith, so that Lachlan across the seas might hear of this legal procedure.

This is the only mention in a legal document that Lachlan in Charles Town was the son of the Captain Ban. At first glance, it is surprising that Farquhar should pay a lawyer for a wild-goose chase, summoning Lachlan in Charles Town - if this was the Indian-trader Lachlan, he lived in Georgia - when the bond in question was guaranteed and repayment was assured at home. Not so surprising though when the lawyer in question was the son of the guarantor and had his own interests to consider.

The document supports the claim that a Lachlan, merchant in Charles Town, was the eldest son of the Captain Ban, and a cousin of Dunmaglass. It is not recorded whether Lachlan settled his father's debts on hearing of these summons, but before long Farquhar would be in Lachlan's debt as fate was smiling more brightly on the M'Gillivrays abroad.

Farquhar managed the affairs of other members of the M'Gillivray clan. In 1751, he acted as cautioner to three unfortunate men, one of them a M'Gillivray from Mamie, who had been picked up in the mountains by a nervous army for carrying arms, then illegal. Not long afterwards, when Alexander M'Gillivray of Mid-Leys sold his lands, Farquhar stepped in as doer. He also had business with Alexander at Knocknagael, and on the latter's death, he claimed for 'wood and other furnishings'. Three years later he negotiated the sale of some property to James Mackintosh of Farr.

Farquhar, the litigator

But some of his deals turned sour. In 1760 he litigated against Thomas Fraser of Gortuleg, one of the trustees of the Lovat Estate. Farquhar claimed that he and Gortuleg had for some time been concerned jointly in the victual trade, buying large quantities of meal and selling it in smaller quantities to people in their country. William Fraser W.S., who recently acted for Farquhar against Lachlan and to whom Gortuleg's son was apprenticed, had bought meal for their joint account from farmers in Petty and Moray but Gortuleg was now refusing to pay his share.

Gortuleg confirmed that in 1756 and 1757, after particularly bad crops, he had bought victual to relieve the distress of the inhabitants of his neighbourhood, but that Dalcrombie had not been involved in the transaction. He flatly denied any partnership with Dalcrombie who, he claimed, had too much unsaleable meal on his hands. He further stated that Dalcrombie bought bear in large quantities because he had a large malting distillery. Gortuleg must have been extremely irritated for he then offered to prove what he said, presumably by leading the excise men to the location of Dalcrombie's distillery.

Despite Dalcrombie's litigious nature and consequent enemies, William of Dunmaglass retained confidence in him and appointed him factor when he joined the army in 1759. Dalcrombie's duties included taking rents from the tenants and litigating if necessary to obtain unpaid sums.

At about this time Dalcrombie's wife died, leaving two young daughters, Isabella and Janet. Farquhar remarried in 1761, to Elizabeth Shaw of Dores, probably of the family of Tordarroch, and Farr reports he had five more children.

The far-from-impartial judiciary system that existed in the 18th century shocks us today. Any man of weight could have another thrown into gaol; if the prisoner had no means, his accuser would meet the food expenses for the duration of the imprisonment. Farquhar asked his friend Duncan Grant, a writer in Inverness, to have Thomas Macpherson, who lived in a neighbouring croft and was planning to emigrate, incarcerated 'for the example'. He was 'of remarkable bad fame; for four years he has been cutting, hashing down and stealing woods of Letterchullin under cloud and influence of night. He had recently stolen cheese and sundry other effects in the neighbourhood; and he is about to elope and leave the country.'

'For the example', Macpherson was apprehended and incarcerated in the Tolbooth of Inverness until Dalcrombie signed his release five months later 'on condition he pay the prison dues'. Whether Thomas Macpherson, whose ancestors (like Dalcrombie's) had cut wood in the forest with impunity, was ever able to emigrate is not known.

It was Dunmaglass, not Farquhar, who engaged in the next process in 1767. Isobel Fraser, the daughter of the Jacobite minister of Daviot, was a Culloden widow of John M'Gillivray, 'natural' son of the Captain Ban. She claimed that her parents were given Ballintruan in Wester Lairgs (Leirgetruan) in life-rent by William's father or grandfather, Farquhar of Dunmaglass. At her father's death, her mother continued in possession but nominally rented the farm to her daughter and son-in-law. Then Dunmaglass' factor and trustee, M'Intosh of Holm, suddenly took it into his head to collect rent, an unjust procedure against a 'poor helpless widow with a small family' whom he wanted to 'force out to beg'.

Dunmaglass now engaged a procedure of removal against this woman, who had been married to his cousin and whose children were his kin. Isobel, with the same gumption as her father, wouldn't go without a fight. She sent her title deeds to the sheriff and claimed that Dunmaglass had never been able to produce his own. But Dunmaglass held that the sasine Isobel produced was unsupported by a warrant and consequently void and null-in-law.

Perhaps Isobel lost her case for in 1784 she applied to the burgh for interest of the £100 that her brother, Thomas Fraser, writer in Edinburgh, had mortified to the town, as well as the mortification left by her uncle, the deceased Robert Fraser, advocate.[37] She obtained the first but not the second that was earmarked for indigent persons residing in the burgh, and Isabel did not qualify.

The purchases of land that Lachlan undoubtedly financed kept Dalcrombie busy. Inverernie was a troublesome acquisition, as for some reason ownership was unclear. Alexander McPhail, accused by Dunmaglass in 1770 of showing a 'new tricks of cunning', continued to enjoy unlawful possession. Dalcrombie eventually had him thrown into the Tolbooth for debt. The McPhails were connected to the M'Gillivrays through the Shaws of Tordarroch; the two families had been close for centuries, living and fighting together, sharing the eldership of the parish kirk – but all neighbourly respect or compassion now vanished. From the Tolbooth, McPhail wrote to William's sister Anne and Dalcrombie (whose Shaw wife was probably his cousin), pleading for a friendly settlement that would be 'wiser, genteeler and of a more Christian disposition'. He continued:

'It was cruel, unjust, unfriendly and unneighbourly to throw me into prison, and not only slander me, but use unfair means for detaining me; and tho' you so much despise my feud or favour, you should consider that the all seeing God knows your Behaviour and will take you to ane account for actions which look so ill in the Eyes of men. Now if you settle with me tomorrow neither Dunmaglass or

---

[37] There do not appear to be more than five mortifications in the 18th century to the poor of Inverness; two of these were from this Fraser family.

any other shall lose a penny by me; if not, as being free of prison is sweet, I must take the benefit of the law for my own liberation, and you and others will lose by my doing so, and Remember that you'll be to blame.'

Christian feelings were laid aside by the M'Gillivrays who now aspired to the wealth and lifestyle that Lachlan possessed and were disposed to use severe methods for an improvement in their fortunes. There was a more serious worry than bankrupting McPhail: the tenants were refusing to pay their rents, pleading ignorance of the true proprietors of the lands. They would not lay their crops without greater security, 'that which Balzebubb would not devise any thing more wicked' as their writer Grant complained in 1774. Grant suggested that Mackintosh of Farr and Dunie should be convened in this matter – this is Dunmaglass surprisingly, who was reportedly across the oceans – and give a poynding to the tenants, or go to the Court of Session on account of 'so many Proprietors and Masters'.

The Inverernie tenants were no longer alone in not paying their rent. Rental default spread to crofts and mills at Gask, Lairgs, Faillie and Dunmaglass: thirty-one of Dunmaglass' tenants were refusing to pay for an unknown reason. Dalcrombie and Anne took legal action to evict them. The tenants included six M'Gillivrays: John Dow and John M'Gillivray in Drumveogy, Benjamin in Milntown of Dunmaglass, Findlay in Clovendale, Farquhar and Archibald's widow in Croachy.

Two years previously, Dr. Samuel Johnson and James Boswell had toured the Highlands, and noted:

'The clans retain little now of their original character. Their ferocity of temper is softened, their military ardour is extinguished, their dignity of independence is depressed, their contempt for government subdued and their reverence for their chierfs abated…As they (the chiefs) gradually degenerate from patriarchal rulers to rapacious landlords, they will divest themselves of the little that remains.'

At the beginning of the century and still even at this period, those with heritable property rarely paid feu-duties to their superiors. In the 1720s, Dunmaglass' father had 'thrown himself at the feet of the

Earl of Moray' pleading for clemencie', which had been granted. His children were now pursuing thirty tenants in more modest condition for lesser sums. Crop failures, inclement weather conditions or the refusal of landlords to improve farmland were to blame, but the root of the problem was land distribution and ownership. The factor took the tenant farmers to court where they were sentenced to pay hefty fines as well as rent arrears. In the 1770s emigration to the New World began in earnest while land proprietors, former chiefs of clans, upped rents and were bent on financial gain.

Dunmaglass would clearly have rated as one of the more oppressive absentee landlords. Nothing is known of the plight of his tenants in arrears and whether the M'Gillivray lands were intentionally being drained of their people.

The long-lasting McPhail saga came to a head several years later when McPhail produced discharges of debt signed by Dunmaglass and Dalcrombie that they denounced as fraudulent, being 'forgeries, fabrications and falsehoods'. He was once again thrown into the Tolbooth. Now well-versed in the law and his rights, McPhail cited the act of King William's parliament whereby 'no person should be imprisoned for any crime or offence without a warrant in writing expressing the particular cause, and the keeper of the prison should immediately give a copy of this warrant to the prisoner, and if this cannot be done within eight days such person is guilty of wrongous imprisonment'. But in mid 1781 he was found guilty, sentenced to life banishment from Scotland and probably transported. Nothing more is known of this chief of the McPhails.

In 1778, there was trouble when Duncan Roy, Jean's husband, tried to evict his co-tenant, John Mor M'Gillivray, perhaps the manager appointed by Lachlan, from part of the lands of Balnagaig. Dalcrombie and Dunmaglass' sister Anne denounced Duncan for making use of their names in this process and held that John had not acquired the lands from them but from Jean, Duncan's spouse 'in whose favour Mr. Lachlan M'Gillivray her brother procured from William M'Gillivray a letter of tack of the town and lands of Balnagaick, exclusive entirely of the said Duncan her husband'. Despite this sanction, William of Dunmaglass ordered payment to be made to him for the education of his children the following year.

Whatever the trouble was between John and Duncan, it was soon resolved, for Duncan fled or died and by 1781 Jean was married to his rival.[38]

Despite Dalcrombie's intractability, he was respected for his skills in the management of the estates Aberchalder, Holm, and in 1770 those of the laird of M'Intosh. His judgment was sought; he was called to adjudicate in disputes, as when Duncan and John M'Gillivrays, both tenants in Balnordan of Aberchalder came to blows over the theft of an axe and a complaint was lodged with the procurator fiscal for the public interest. He was also chosen to pronounce on a question of marches in the lands of Tullich and Elrig between M'Intoshes of Aberarder and Moy.

The Dalcrombies lived at the homestead of Letterchullin, on the lofty tree-covered bank of Loch Duntelchaig, and records show that Farquhar or his son Donald was in 1777 also tacksman of the farm of Drumboy.[39]

Farquhar and his daughter Janet's husband, Michael M'Gillivray (of unknown parentage) were partners in different business deals and soon acquired a reputation for avarice and deviousness. In 1788, Kyllachy's factor, James M'Intosh at Garbol, defended one William M'Gillivray and his daughter who shared the farmlands of Faillie with Michael and his wife.[40] William, who owed Michael a sum of money, sold him his crop. Once the crop was safely in Michael's possession and before paying, Michael sued his co-tenant for the money owing and raised a process of 'multiple poinding' against William's creditors. M'Intosh was either one of these creditors or was moved to act from sheer indignation; he defended his friend and accused Farquhar of Dalcrombie and Michael of 'adopting every plan which ingenuity can suggest in

---

[38] Simon Fraser Mackintosh though makes John her only husband, with her children from this marriage.

[39] The will of a Mrs. Isabel M'Gillivray, who died in Inverness in 1779, leaving £34 in cash, mentions Donald, tenant in Drumboy, Farquhar, resident in Inverness and Ann M'Gillivray, widow of the deceased Alexander Dallas, tenant in Culduthall. Cautioner was Farquhar M'Gillivray of Dalcrombie. Perhaps this Isabel was one of Farquhar's relatives.

[40] In 1779, this farm apparently belonged to Dunmaglass' sister Catherine. William and his daughter moved to Dell or Morle.

order to withhold the payment of the corn and straw (...) and to oppress their namesake William M'Gillivray (:...) It appears however that this gentleman, Mr. M'Gillivray (Dalcrombie), though in opulent circumstances, is not one of those who is fond to part with his money... All the while he, Michael, holds in his hands the very funds that he admits to be due. The plan of the multiple poinding is exceedingly improper operated between the father and son-in--law in collusion....'

Underhand acquisition of Abercalder

Farquhar made enemies. He was active, if not the agent, in the feud that divided the M'Gillivray sisters of Aberchalder, a property near Dunmaglass that had belonged to this M'Gillivray family for generations. In 1736, their mother Anne, daughter of the Dalzeil of Petty family and sister of Alexander of the Carolinas, married Alexander of Aberchalder. The couple had two daughters, and abandoning hope of ever having a son and to prevent their property going to a male relation when the father died, disponed it to the elder daughter Janet and any heirs of her body, with her sister Anne next-in-line. Janet would soon marry Captain Alexander Fraser of Bunchegovie, and have at least one son. But a late child was born to the fortunate Aberchalder couple: Martin, the long-awaited son and heir, and presumably the earlier sale was revoked for he inherited from his father. Farquhar of Dalcrombie was tutor and factor to the child when his father died, and was responsible for uplifting rents. Aberchalder was a small but beautiful estate nestling under the mountains. It produced little more than £50 a year, from which it paid a feu duty of £14 to the Earl of Moray and an annuity of £15 to Alexander's widow. Alas, Martin died young and elder sister Janet inherited in 1778 after all, according to her father's will. She sold the estate to John Fraser, tenant farmer in Garthmore, probably a relative of her husband, Captain Alexander Fraser of Garthmore, now at Bunchegovie.

But Dalcrombie coveted the property, either for himself or for his rich Dunmaglass cousin Colonel John, for whom he was doer. Together with William of Dunmaglass and Janet's sister Anne, he seems to have menaced Janet with the danger of a male heir in

America and his claim to the property, which, if successful, would mean she would get nothing. Privately, he admitted the American heir had a weak case. But faced with the prospect of long litigation, Janet applied for the property to be sequestered and a factor appointed by court as there was an arrear of feu-duties due by Dalcrombie to the Earl of Moray who was threatening to take legal action. Farquhar felt this to be a slur on his probity and retorted that the Earl of Moray 'demanded more and more'; as factor for a minor he did not feel authorised to accept an increase.

'Their meaning,' wrote Farquhar ominously of Janet and her advisors 'is easily seen through, they would in a dark and sly way endeavour to convey to your Lordships an idea of mismanagement on the part of Dalcrombie whom they dare not attack in a more open manner.'

A compromise was eventually found with Dalcrombie and Janet's sister Anne; now the two sisters were cited as co-heiresses to their brother Martin. John Fraser, who had earlier bought the land and was holding out for his entitlement, died in the middle of the proceedings in 1781 so the sale was cancelled and there was no obstacle. The next day, the sisters sold their estate to Farquhar of Dalcrombie, and there was no more mention of the American male heir. Whose funds were used to acquire the property is unclear. Anne was rewarded: although the property was no longer hers, she was allowed to continue its occupation. Later Farquhar sold the estate to Colonel John, and he too was rewarded: if John and his heirs died without issue, the property would revert to Dalcrombie or his issue. The losing party in this litigation was of course young Fraser of Bunchegovie.

William of Dunmaglass had a close relationship with Dalcrombie. From the little correspondence that survives between the two men it is apparent that Dunmaglass was fond of and respected his older cousin. He asks his opinion on political events in Britain, and ends his letters with the closing 'affectionately'. William's younger brother Colonel John, a business man, is more abrupt, chastising Dalcrombie when he acted without consulting him first, but willing to help the family out by lending funds to pay his brother's debts.[41] There is no surviving correspondence between Dalcrombie and Lachlan, but when Lachlan is mentioned in letters to the brothers, Dalcrombie refers to him respectfully as 'Mr. Lachlan'.

---

[41] His identity is not known although the Farr Manuscript records a brother named Alexander.

CHAPTER FOUR
LEGAL INTRICACIES

Lachlan and Colonel John in America

When it was clear that their fortunes and future in America were no longer secure and that Savannah would be taken by the revolutionary forces and the Loyalists banished, Colonel John, recovering from his Mississippi adventure and then imprisonment in Cuba (1778-1780), joined Lachlan to discuss their situation. Lachlan decided he would return to Scotland, but he did not want to return as a man of means. Lachlan and John came to what Dr. E. Cashin terms 'an unusual agreement'.[42] Lachlan turned over his extensive property to Colonel John in exchange for an annuity of £500. Vale Royal and twenty-two other properties were transferred to John's name in September 1781.

What pushed Lachlan, a lucid man of business, to put his whole fortune in another's hands? He had a lifetime record of good judgment and commercial and political acumen. If he was eldest son of the Captain Ban, he was second in line to Dunmaglass as long as the present Dunmaglass brothers had no male heirs. Lachlan's own son, a half-breed American, could not succeed. If there was an American nephew, son of Alexander, he was now heir apparent to Dunmaglass. Was Lachlan's action intended to disinherit his brother's son because he had no wish for this young man, his next-of-kin, to serve heir?

Perhaps by now, in 1781, he was generally recognized to be the Captain Ban's son. But suppose he was not. He would return with the identity of this cousin of Dunmaglass and upon his demise unknown heirs - his attributed siblings Farquhar, Charles, William, Alexander, Louisa and Emilia or their children - might successfully claim the fortune made by Lachlan, undesirable heirs for they were not his kin. Even if he left a will, the estate of Dunmaglass, which

---

[42] *Lachlan McGillivray, Indian Trader. The Shaping of the Southern Colonial Frontier*

had been improved and extended with the funds made from 'labour and fatigue of a number of years spent in a disagreeable climate and frequently exposed to dangers', as William of Dunmaglass put it, would not go to the heirs of his choice.

If this was the reason, it was veiled. Lachlan later cited instead his 'years and infirmities' for making the decision. His withdrawal from an active business life marked the beginning of many changes within this M'Gillivray family. Assets would be taken to other parts of the world and held in other hands. Most significantly, William of Dunmaglass was married and had a daughter. But for the time being, thanks to Lachlan, Colonel John was at the head of a small empire in America, England (where he also had property) and Scotland.

Colonel John assumed ownership of Vale Royal, and he and Lachlan were joined here by a relative from Scotland, twenty-year old Lachlan, two of whose brothers were already in America. He was the youngest son of Archibald in Daviot, and according to the traditional genealogies, a very remote relation of the older Lachlan. He managed the estates of his relations for a short time before Savannah surrendered to American troops. Loyalists were given six months to settle their business affairs and in May 1782, the older Lachlan sailed for England. In spite of his arrangement with Colonel John, his estates were confiscated by the Georgia General Assembly.

Lachlan had spent forty years of his life in the New World; he had a common-law wife and at least three children, Alexander, Janet and Sophia and perhaps another daughter, Sehoy. There were also grandchildren and numerous friends in both the Anglo-Scottish and Indian communities. His forced departure must have been painful yet he does not seem to have hesitated about returning to his homeland.

Colonel John made arrangements to save what he could of his property. In June 1782 he bought the brig Prince William Henry lying in Savannah harbour to transport his slaves to Jamaica. This was an island where many Scots had gone in earlier times in search of 'prodigious riches'. Sir Alexander Grant, son of Lydia M'Intosh of Borlum, owned 10,000 acres of plantation land before moving to London where he was one of the leading merchants of the time.

Colonel John would not have been a stranger to trade with the West Indies. Jamaica and East Florida were already linked under another great merchant and financier, the Scot Richard Oswald, who supplied American planters with provisions, 'often before the planters knew that they needed it'. Their greatest need was manpower. By 1770 Oswald had sent to East Florida three ships laden with slave cargo from his slave factory in Sierra Leone. In exchange, he imported and sold planters' crops, chiefly indigo.

Colonel John was among the last Loyalists to leave Georgia. With Governor Wright as fellow passenger, he sailed for Jamaica in April 1783. Some provision had already been made by the Crown that allotted land, albeit insalubrious, along Black River in St. Elizabeth's parish, to one hundred and eighty-two Loyalist applicants. Among them were the three M'Gillivrays: Colonel John, Lachlan, and Lachlan (Jr.). The worthless lands, too expensive to drain, included what ten years previously had been described locally as fit for no living creature, except 'fish, frogs, Dutchmen and amphibious animals'. Colonel John did not stay long in Jamaica. He left Lachlan Jr. to oversee the slaves near Black River and find a better estate. By July, he was at Tavistock in England ('14 miles this side of Plymouth' he wrote north to Scotland) with his brother William and relative Lachlan.[43]

William's arrangements

William had left Savannah and managed, with difficulty, to return to London in advance of his relations. Soon afterwards he married Joanna of the Mackenzies of Fairburn, then living in Barking near London. This was in early 1779.

About this time, Farquhar of Dalcrombie was contemplating using the male heir to block the sale of Aberchalder that he meant for himself or his Dunmaglass cousins. It appears from a letter that William wrote back to Dalcrombie from London that the male heir was in Carolina, that William knew him, perhaps corresponded with

---

[43] Curiously, another John M'Gillivray lived very close by; he was a teacher at Lostwithiel School which in 1778 moved to Bodmin; this John had earlier been a master at Eton. A sample of his poetry is at the British Library, London.

him, and that Archibald at Daviot would have remembered his grandfather whose name was William:

London, Sept 9th 1779

Dear Cousin,

Social reasons and among others my not being in good spirits prevented my writing you and some others for some time past. There is at present a Terrible Cloud hanging over the affairs of this Kingdom and of course those of America. I concluded some time ago that Carolina would long ere now be in the hands of Government but that prospect is now distant indeed, if not out of sight. Till that happens no access can be had to the male Heir of Aberchaladar who by the by is silly enough and would not risque a shilling unless sure of success, which according to your state is more than doubtful. However, if you are determined to try it and that you will procure me the proper directions or steps that the Heir male ought to take to ascertain his Claim, my part in the matter will not be wanting. In the meantime, Daviot's Evidence should be taken which may lead a little and prove serviceable in both Countries. I hope your Reversion in case the younger sister should die without Heirs of her own body will prove good.

I would not myself like to trust to irritant Clauses where a man made a disposition and had a Right to make it. If there are any others besides Daviot that remember this William Grandfather to the present Heir male his Evidence should be taken as it will give great weight in Carolina. My time is not known to myself therefore no time ought to be lost. I am very happy that your son William is turned a stout fellow and pretty far advanced in his Education. I have made Enquiry at different agents and offices and find that there would not be much difficulty in getting him a Commission agreeable to the rules laid down by General Lord Amhurst but there is little hope of his departing from any of them. (…)

I had at the same time promises which are still depending to get letters of recommendation to the Commander in Chief in America to appoint me to the Command. If I could form a Corps of Americans in which case I might be able to have him at home to prosecute his studies. Lord Amhurst told me if more Regiments are to be raised in this Country, he will if agreeable recommend me to the King. What is your opinion? I believe there will be no more, but that depends on events. I have stated the matter with regard to you for so far as my knowledge extends and expect your own sentiments as soon as possible. William MacKintosh Balnespick has agreeable to the above Rule purchased a Lieut. Colonelcy for £1000 Sterling. My sister Kathy wrote me that you expected her to account for her farms of £10 in Faillie and some trifle of money advanced her and sister Beatty. You are to have credit in your Intromission for what it may be.

Draw on Mr. John Simsons of Hellon Court, Threadtheneedle Street, London for £50 sterling to be applied for the Relief of Education of Duncan Roy's family. Another year will produce some certainty of better or worse. Therefore you should give Jean and her family serious and good advice. Is the Laird of Mackintosh £200 in my Debt yet? Grant at Edin £100 I suppose paid. The list of Debts you sent me expected to be paid at Martinmas first is £789.16.6. Wilham Cuthbert's £100 I suppose you have already intimated the payment of. Lieut. Fraser will likewise receive his £100. As I expect My Brother John home I would wish to put of (sic) the rest of the List to March next tho I have but little doubt if any of the parties are pressing but they will receive their payment at Martinmas, but I am not inclined to promise so much. Let me know their sentiments. Grant's, Cuthbert's and Fraser's will amount to £900 off this year. (…)[44]

We wonder what serious and good advice Dalcrombie would give Jean and her family, and what subject the certainty referred to. We

---

[44] National Archives of Scotland, GD 128/23/6/58 (part) - extracts

should note that only part of the letter has survived; it would have been telling to know how the letter ended. That William complained of a busy social life is understandable; that he should have been in poor spirits only a few months into his marriage is troubling.

Instead of pursuing a more active military career as hoped, he joined an invalid company of soldiers at Plymouth on account of an injured tendon. Here, a daughter Barbara was born in 1781. Her baptism is registered in the parish records. Then on 16 October 1782, son John Lachlan was born. His baptism was not recorded.[45] There is no further mention of Joanna, who must have died in childbirth.

Instead of being on his way to England as William expected, Colonel John was languishing in a Havana prison. He only returned to England in the summer of 1783, after accompanying his slaves to Jamaica. In Devon, he found Lachlan, newly arrived from America, 'fat and hearty' but his brother William very ill. With them was William's sister Anne. Lachlan and Colonel John helped William draw up an official claim for his confiscated American estate. He also made out a will in favour not of his children, but of his brother. Despite taking a goat milk cure in Abergaveny in Wales, considered at the time of medicinal value, his state deteriorated. Colonel John thought the goats' milk at Dunmaglass was of better quality, that the sea air would revive his brother, and planned to accompany him to Scotland on a visit.

In a letter from London to Farquhar of Dalcrombie at the end of July, Colonel John wrote of his surprise that Farquhar had bought Aberchalder for him: 'I suppose the reason of such a purchase was being long in possession of our Name adjoining Dunmaglass. Mrs. Aberchalder, when alive and her daughter Miss Anne being enthusiastically fond of its continuing were no doubt strong inducements (…) £1800 I am told is what is to be paid for it.' But Colonel John was badly informed. Although some money would be handed over three months later, there was on-going litigation concerning who had inherited from brother Martin and who was

---

[45] Date of birth given by Simon Fraser Mackintosh. John Lachlan's birthplace was reported as Plymouth in the 1851 census.

entitled to sell. The question would not be resolved for another year – and until then Aberchalder could not change hands.

Colonel John added that he had written to his brother William to inform him that he would pay off all the debts on his estate. As there were no legal liens from creditors on Dunmaglass, the nature of these debts is unknown, the money owing mentioned in the 1779 letter being well below the value of all Dunmaglass' estates. Subsequently, however, these debts would turn out to be of great significance.

The plans to venture north did not materialize; neither did William's health improve. On his son's first birthday on 16 October 1783, weak and infirm in body, but of disposing mind, William signed a last deed nominating tutors for his infant children and disposed of his earthly goods through the courts of Canterbury. He then packed his bags in Plymouth, bid farewell to the children, and sailed, ailing and perhaps alone, to Portugal where the winter was milder. But whatever ailment he had could not be cured in more clement weather; he died in Lisbon a few weeks later in November 1783, leaving two orphans aged one and two.

William's testament does not shed light on the convoluted financial arrangements between the different M'Gillivrays. It refers to a settlement that Colonel John had made on Barbara Ann that would mature when she was 21 or when she married, and her father now added a further annual £50 to this sum. Then it refers at great length to the purchase that Colonel John had made of Aberchalder in his name. In exchange for Aberchalder, William now gave Colonel John his lands of Faillie, bought with American money, and Gask that he himself had inherited and would not be leaving to his own son.

He thus gave away properties in exchange for Aberchalder which he never got. Dalcrombie handed over £900 to the Frasers of Bunchegovie 'on behalf of Dunmaglass' a whole year later, and ten days before the latter died, for a receipt that wasn't registered in the book of deeds. William's assertion that Aberchalder was his or Colonel John's was therefore jumping the gun. Janet Fraser and Anne M'Gillivray were only served heirs to their brother in May 1784, and it was only then that they sold – but not to Colonel John. The purchaser was Farquhar of Dalcrombie. Yet when William made out his will, he took great pains to state that only Colonel John and his heirs would get his lands to the exclusion of any other heirs that he, William, might have. Concerning Colonel John and his heirs, he wrote:

'All right title or interest which I have in these lands be by him or them for ever after quietly and peaceably held and enjoyed and in case that he or they shall at anytime hereafter be molested and interrupted in the quiet and peaceable enjoyment of the same by any person or persons who maybe intitled to any benefit or interest under this my last will and testament that such person or persons shall forfeit and lose all such benefit, interest and advantage and I do in such case substitute and appoint my said brother John and his heirs or assignees to receive and take the same to his or their own use and behoof as a recompense and compensation to him or them for the loss and injury which he or they will sustain by reason that the agreement aforesaid between us hath not been carried into execution according to our true and real intent and meaning and I do hereby declare that it is my will that the quiet enjoyment of the said two pieces or parcels of land called Faillie and Gask by my said brother John, his heirs and assignees shall be considered as a condition precedent to any benefit, interest or advantage to be held or taken under this my last will and testament, by any person or person whatever who under any pretence may endeavour to interrupt or prevent the same.'

The only obstruction to his will would appear to be from legitimate children who were older than John Lachlan, but there don't seem to be any. William's daughter Barbara Ann was his residual heir, while his son would get 'the rest', to include any future compensation for his American lands. There was not much left in fact to give: only Dunmaglass, which, according to Colonel John, was heavily burdened in his favour. In reality then, Dunmaglass left nothing to John Lachlan, except perhaps the posthumous compensation for his American rice-fields. The executors to his last will and testament and guardians of the children until the age of 21 were his brother Colonel John, his sister Anne and his cousin Lachlan. Probate of the will was granted in the Court of Canterbury on 29 January 1784 and the following year put in the hands of George Bean, Notary Publick in Inverness.

Compensation claims

If the young children now came back to Inverness, they would have arrived in the middle of a severe famine: this was the year of the white pease, when the crops failed and food was imported from Holland. Sheriff Simon Fraser in Inverness was in charge of its distribution; Captain John M'Intosh clamoured for more for his Kyllachy tenants, William M'Gillivray at the Inn of Dalmagarry was in charge of the quota for Moy. From London, where Lachlan was staying with Ann and Colonel John, Lachlan remitted £600, a considerable sum, through John to unnamed nieces. In March 1784, Lachlan and John deposited their claims, together with two posthumous ones from William, with the 'Commissioners appointed by Act of Parliament to deal with the claims of the American Loyalists'.

Backing the claims were statements from Governor Sir James Wright and Lt-Governor John Graham. In his statement, Lachlan declared that he found himself less capable to manage and take care of his affairs in America 'which required a good deal of care and attention'. Also he had suffered much 'persecution and vexation for his attachment to his Majesty's Government and being therefore desirous to extricate himself from the distress and perplexity he had laboured under in consequence of the troubles, he made overtures to his nephew John M'Gillivray who he considered was his heir as he, Lachlan, was never married, to give up to the said John immediately what the deponent intended the said John should receive at his death, to wit, all the lands, houses and real estates in Georgia belonging to the deponent, upon the said John securing to the deponent an annuity competent to support him during the term of his natural life.'

On oath, Lachlan said that he was 65 and that John was his nephew - not his cousin. Lachlan was born in 1718 or 1719 and was therefore not the son of Farquhar of Dunmaglass (dead by 1714) and not Colonel John's paternal uncle if John was of the Dunmaglass family.

William's petition stated that he had gone to America at the desire of a cousin german[46] who had promised to make him his heir[47], that when leaving Georgia in order to return to Britain to join up in the army he had been in Charles Town 'in the most disagreeable situation imaginable, obliged to wait for a passage to Europe for near 12 months, which was frequently refused him on account of his difference in sentiment, at the same time that it was often signified to him how offensive and even dangerous his appearance was, and that he sometimes met with insult and ill treatment'. His account ends lamely: he had an estate in the Highlands of Scotland, where he was likewise the head of a clan, and were he in the army again he would hold the rank of Lieutenant Colonel.

A second, unsigned, memorial differs, saying that he was not in fact a colonel but a captain in the Invalid Forces, because soon after his arrival in England he had the misfortune to break the great tendon of his leg, which made him unfit for very active duty.

William claimed £11,098, and apparently received £2,890 in compensation; Colonel John received £9,048 of £27,462 claimed, which was the average of one third paid by the Crown.[48] John also possessed a plantation and slaves in Jamaica, other unidentified assets in England, and the estates his brother had given him in Scotland. But it was not enough. Soon after the depositions he, Anne and Lachlan went northwards to their friends and relations in Inverness, Colonel John to a homeland he may not have seen since his departure thirty years previously. His visit was marked by the forceful legal steps he took to secure the last property that belonged to his deceased brother that he deemed was his – Dunmaglass itself. But the times when a M'Gillivray could hold that he was head of a clan - as William had so abjectly done in his compensation claim - were long since gone.

---

[46] First cousin and more specifically having the same grandparents on either the maternal or paternal side. A second memorial from William calls Lachlan a near relation.

[47] A similar promise had earlier been made to John.

[48] Amos Wright.

The Infant in litigation

Lachlan, Colonel John and his sister Anne, all of them elderly, were left to look after William's orphaned infants.[49] They returned to Scotland, to their town house in Inverness and the summer home of Dunmaglass.

Friends and relations in the north would have had difficulty keeping up with the changes occurring in the family's circumstances. Dalcrombie was again litigating and the Frasers, the defenders, expressed their bewilderment as regards the true proprietor of Dunmaglass.[50] In 1778 William's sister Anne and Dalcrombie had turned to the courts over the peat marshes of the Moss of Blairmore between the Fraser properties of Torbreak and Culduthel and the M'Gillivray property of Gask. Both families held that their tenants since time immemorial had been cutting these peats for use in their hearths and for sale to the people of Inverness, and both sides claimed that the other's tenants were encroaching on their rights.

Despite an adjudicator trying to appease both parties with new boundaries between their properties, the quarrel trailed on through the years and was only settled in 1788. The M'Gillivrays lost their action, and were found liable to the defenders in expenses. Both sets of tenants continued to cut their peat from the Moss of Blairmore as though no pronouncement on ownership had ever been made.

But let us look more closely at some of the details. In the early 1780s, the Frasers questioned the right of Farquhar of Dalcrombie and Anne M'Gillivray (by then joined by Colonel John) to act in the name of Dunmaglass, and referred to their 'want of title'. Worse, they seemed not to know who their old neighbour, the late Dunmaglass was, and demanded a legal submission of an account of his life and movements, which was thus drawn up:

---

[49] It is curious that one of Joanna's relations, presumably her sister, (married to Charles Graham of London, one of the children's curators) who also had young children, did not raise her nephew. Barbara Ann may well have stayed with her for she was educated not in the Highlands but in Greenwich.

[50] Co-litigant was Colonel Duncan Macpherson of Bleaton, William's neighbour in Wester Gask and fellow officer in Captain Long Morris' Regiment.

'The late Captain William M'Gillivray, of Dunmaglass, was born in the year 1732, and his father (blank) M'Gillivray of Dunmaglass departed this life in June 1740, when his son was no more than eight years of age; whereby there was a minority of thirteen years, which ended in the year 1753. In the year 1759, the said Captain M'Gillivray, after recruiting his company of men, which engrossed his attention for some time, went to the East Indies, where he was for sundry years; and indeed, after his return therefrom, he soon went to America and England, where he remained till within a few weeks of his death, which happened in November 1783, at Lisbon, where he had gone for his health.'

From this account, it would appear that Dunmaglass had not been in the vicinity for a considerable time, and his activities for seven years, between 1765 when his regiment disbanded and 1772 when he went to America, seem to be unknown or fudged by the writers. Free-mason records show that William was in Inverness circa 1770 when he was Master of the Inverness Lodge. Another legal document notes that the petition was made by Farquhar of Dalcrombie and Miss Anne, 'sister-german of Captain William of Dunmaglass and of the said Farquhar', which we presume is a scribal error.

When the Frasers learnt that Captain William was dead, they then addressed the owner of Gask as 'the infant, the supposed proprietor of the lands' and 'the infant gentleman'. Only in 1785 were Farquhar, Anne and Colonel John able to present the Settlement and Deed of Nomination drawn up three years previously by William and deposited at the Court of Canterbury to prove 'the infant's' entitlement.

Lachlan and Colonel John apparently settled at Dunmaglass, together with Anne. This was a temporary residence for John, who meant Gask for his home; this had been left to him by his brother William. It was the farmstead of the Dunmaglass children, where the rebels in the 1746 sharpened their broadswords before the fateful battle of Culloden. Perhaps he himself had watched the preparations. Colonel John instructed Dalcrombie to improve and furnish the farm and hire servants, in readiness for his return from Jamaica where he now planned to go.

First though, Colonel John needed to get Aberchalder for the infant John Lachlan in exchange for Gask. For a year now it had been in the name of Farquhar of Dalcrombie. In March 1785, Colonel John and Farquhar settled their accounts, and, on paper at least, Colonel John became owner of the stately farm of Aberchalder despite an outstanding balance of £400 that he agreed to pay Dalcrombie within a few days. The contract of sale gave Farquhar of Dalcrombie and his heirs entitlement to the property if neither John Lachlan nor his sister had issue.

In the summer of 1785, the orphaned children were perhaps taken to the homestead at Dunmaglass, where Colonel John and Anne were staying, and where Lachlan planned reforestation for the surrounding lands. The son of the innkeeper at Dalmagarry, William M'Gillivray, who was blind and knew about dogs, was instructed to secure two pointer puppies for the children. When the first heavy snows made the property inaccessible and remote, the family and their baggage were brought back by chaise to their Inverness townhouse for the long winter. Their close friends included Dr. William Kennedy as well as the young Walcot family. Captain Thomas Walcot had remarried after the death of his wife Betsy Fraser.[51] His new wife, Marjory, was the children's aunt, their mother's sister. Their family now comprised one daughter, Edmondina, two years younger than John Lachlan, and the children of Captain Walcot's first marriage, Thomas and Jane, born probably in Gibraltar. Did John Lachlan, who had no mother, cast his eyes with childish wonder on this gentle step-cousin, five years his senior? As soon as he was of age, they would marry – but this was still in the unforeseeable future.

Colonel John's affairs were very complicated. After the summer spent at Dunmaglass, he went south to Edinburgh to confer with his lawyer, Charles M'Intosh, where he received a letter from Dalcrombie to inform him that the firs were being planted, and that the heavy snow would at least preserve them from the deadly frost. Dalcrombie was buying clothes for the servants at Gask, but 'all the laws of Scotland will not recover money from tenants in this country. I plainly foresee we shall again first Whitsunday have a

---

[51] He was Master of St. Andrew's Kilwinning in 1782, 1790 and 1796

good deal of lands without tenants and really its better having lands lay than possessed by such miserable and obstinate creatures.' He added that by mistake he had opened some of Col John's letters that arrived at Baillie McIntosh's shop in the belief that they dealt with business but they were about private matters 'the import shall be a dead secret as to me, leave you to judge the contents…'

But Colonel John was not content with the prospect of a quiet life in Gask. He had taken over all of Lachlan's properties in America and paid him a stipend in exchange. He now sought to attach the totality of William's properties 'as there was a debt owing to him from the representatives of his brother exceeding the value of his whole estate in Scotland'. With some foresight before travelling to Jamaica, a dangerous country with its insalubrious climate, he drew up a will in which he made his nephew John Lachlan his heir.

Then Colonel John and Charles M'Intosh instituted legal proceedings against his nephew's guardians, that is to say against himself, Lachlan and Anne. To complicate our understanding of the motives behind this and pointing to the possibility that this might not be a matter of mere formality, the summons of Adjudication in April 1787 would chastise John Lachlan for delaying in entering heir to his father and state he had not paid the 'the balance of a particular account…so the lands should be adjudged as belonging to John M'Gillivray and Charles M'Intosh, his representative'. No details about the accounts between the two parties have survived. Rev. Lachlan, the claimant at the 1850s litigation, put it very aptly seventy years later: Colonel John successfully executed a disposition and conveyance of the family estates without ever having acquired any title thereto.

There is an undated note: 'Principal sum and interest from 12 April to 24 July 1787, being one year 103 days £11,591.5.9 3/4d. Make it £11,590, neglecting the odd £1.5.9d.' The note means payment rather than a book-keeping entry.

Colonel John had been scarcely a year in Jamaica, attending to his slaves and the building of a new home, Sunflower estate, when he caught a tropical disease. He boarded a vessel to return to England in 1787, but died just one day into the sea journey and was presumably buried at sea. Although he would have been younger than his brother Captain William who was born in 1732, he had had a hard and adventurous life, and is referred to in correspondence from his attorney in Jamaica as an 'old gentleman'.

Who got the settlement of adjudication against William's heirs that John Lachlan's tutors had to make in 1789? It would appear that nobody did: what one hand paid out, the other took back. John Lachlan was both payor and payee. Colonel John had simply reversed the situation to its former state after what appears to be a senseless and expensive procedure. The note rounding down the sum of money for transfer and the continuation of the process of adjudication when Colonel John had died are therefore incomprehensible. The only beneficiary and receptacle into which all these accounts spilt their interest like cream or honey was the infant John Lachlan, who was - this much seems clear - heir to everyone as things stood. There was no need for any legal procedure.

There was recondite correspondence from Colonel John's solicitor, Charles M'Intosh in Edinburgh to Charles Graham of London (very likely the children's maternal uncle by marriage) dated June 1788, that was produced at the litigation:

'You know that the transactions betwixt the Col. and Dunmaglass were exceedingly loose. Dunmaglass was largely indebted to his brother, and was to have sold him a part of his land in Scotland. But no proper deeds were executed so as to vest the property in the Colonel, neither did Dunmaglass himself execute any deed to regular the succession of his lands in this country; so that if the Colonel and Dunmaglass's son were both to die before the son came of age, the lands would go to a channel that neither the Col. nor the other friends of the family would approve of. The Colonel wrote me from London on this subject, and I advised him to make his debt a real burden upon his brother's estate, by raising what we call a decreet of adjudication against it; and although he could not make a deed that would regulate the succession of the estate, he could do what would be tantamount, by giving the adjudication (which would be of greater value than the estate) to whomsoever he pleased.

In consequence of this adjudication, and the Col.'s settlement, Dunmaglass' son is now a real creditor (by what is equivalent to a mortgage over his father's whole property in Scotland), to the extent of £11,500 sterling, bearing interest from the 24th of July 1787. This not only covers the estate from all unknown American claims, but also, in the event of the child's death, prevents the danger of its going to a remote heir-male, and sends it in the channel that Dunmaglass himself and the Col. wished it to go. I do not know whether I have made myself perfectly intelligible. But if you wish any further explanation, I shall give every satisfaction in my power.'

Colonel John's wishes, referred to by his lawyer, were detailed in his Deed of Settlement. The properties were entailed in the following order: his own male issue (apparently none), John Lachlan and his male issue (they would inherit Aberchalder even before Colonel John's issue), Colonel John's female issue (apparently none), John Lachlan's female issue, Barbara and her issue, Lachlan's heirs of his body (apparently there was no legitimate issue) and finally Farquhar of Dalcrombie's issue. In the event of John Lachlan's premature death, Dunmaglass, which could only be inherited by a male heir, would therefore go to Dalcrombie's issue.

Closer heirs-at-law that were being cut out were the sons of David in Ballintruan, and any descendants of the Captain Ban and his brother Donald in Inverness, if there were any. The families of Alexander in Knocknagael and Archibald in Daviot that wouldn't seem to take precedence in any case over Farquhar of Dalcromby's line – but this may not have been clear at the time - were also being tacity excluded. All or some of these constituted 'undesirable channel(s)' or 'remote heirs-male'.

Were these the real considerations behind this adjudication? And were there really any American heirs? Alexander of the Creek Nation and Colonel John's Métis children would not have been recognised as lawful issue. On the other hand, any children of the Captain Ban's children, or the Dunmaglass brothers, in America or elsewhere, would have been lawful heirs – but not before the child

John Lachlan.[52] John Lachlan's position could only be challenged by older sons that William may have had, or if John Lachlan's paternity was contested. Both these hypotheses seem valid. One might easily construe the existence of older children from William's will and Charles M'Intosh's guarded language. Any older sons had no claim on his properties. And, as the lawyer pointed out, Colonel John could give the Adjudication to whomever he pleased. Giving it to John Lachlan suggests that he was not in the right position to begin with. Whatever the case, these arrangements appear to cover the existence of separate families, separate heirs, hidden IOUs and ultimately changed genealogies.

Despite or on account of all these procedures, John Lachlan was declared heir to his father and uncle in 1790. The same year he obtained title to the lands of Easter Aberchalder that carried a seat desk in the church of Daviot and Dunlichity. Two years later he became owner of Faillie, Wester Lairgs and the Easter half of Gask. He appears to have inherited these lands from his father and not his uncle, which suggests that neither William's will at the Prerogative Court of Canterbury nor Colonel John's attempt to attach his brother's property succeeded. The following year John Lachlan obtained title, as heir to his father, to the oldest M'Gillivray property of all – Dunmaglass.

The end of an era

Lachlan lived to an old age, moving every spring from the Inverness house to Dunmaglass, and back again in the autumn. Like others in affluent circumstances, Lachlan donated to good causes: a new steeple for the town church and the new Inverness Academy. In 1788 he was one of thirteen gentlemen who met at the Town Hall in Inverness to found the Northern Meeting, an annual event with piping, dancing and games. At Dunmaglass he oversaw reforestation of ash and birch woods, and at Faillie the great black wood. He

---

[52] Hugh Swinton McGillivray of Charleston claimed descent from Lachlan's brother, Alexander. The registered will of an Alexander, sea mariner in Charleston, with a brother Lachlan, mentions a wife but no child. Amos Wright gives Hugh Swinton M'Gillivray a different ancestry.

ordered around and used the Dunmaglass tenants, writing to his factor: 'I desire that you all send Monday first notice to Fraser to order the tenants to be at Inverness on Thursday first with eight horses to bring up here four bols of shell lime for the house and a large barn.'

When John Lachlan ('Johnny') recovered from some illness, Lachlan wrote to Campbell M'Intosh, town clerk depute of Inverness: 'Blessed be God for his mercys.'[53] On another occasion, Lachlan wrote to him: 'I wish to see Johnny here with me if it should be but for a week or ten days...'

In a surprising development, Captain William of Dunmaglass' sister Anne, while apparently living with Lachlan and her nephew, sued the latter for unpaid debts in her favour. The last document she signed in March 1790 was to recognise John Lachlan as heir to her brother. She died a few weeks later. She left no will although she was now owed a tidy sum. Her personal effects - including a gold watch with chain, a gold hairpin, a miniature picture of Colonel John, three gold rings and sets of earrings - were given to her niece. John Lachlan got nothing as, according to the lawyers, his half was 'more than compensated by heritable bonds and others'.

Lachlan was now John Lachlan's only surviving guardian. He quickly appointed other tutors to share the task: Charles Graham in London, who was perhaps married to a maternal aunt, William M'Intosh of Aberarder and Bailie William Inglis, merchant in Inverness. Campbell M'Intosh, also a tutor, took over from Dalcrombie as factor.[54] Their duties lasted until the children turned fourteen, when the law required that curators should be appointed. This appointment meant that in January 1798 John Lachlan, then at St Andrew's University, and Barbara Ann, living in Greenwich, had to summon their nearest-of-kin, namely Alexander in Ballindruan (who was their father's cousin) and Jean, spouse of John Mor M'Gillivray in Balnagacek on their father's side, and Mrs. Marjory Mackenzie, spouse of Captain Walcot, and Mrs. Barbara McKenzie,

---

[53] Campbell M'Intosh was of the M'Intosh of Aberarder branch. He was born in 1758 in Delnies, Nairn; his godmother was one Jean M'Gillivray.

[54] A few years later, Campbell M'Intosh was able to borrow £500 from Colonel John's executors (he also being one of them) to widen the streets and lanes of Inverness.

relict of the deceased Kenneth Murchison, Esquire of Tarradale, on their mother's side, 'to hear and see curators' election'. Barbara Mackenzie, who lived in Newtown of Edinburgh, was excused from the task as she lived outside the jurisdiction.[55]

The former tutors now became curators, together with Simon Fraser of Farraline, advocate and sheriff depute of Inverness, and John McIntosh, Provost.

More land had been acquired with family funds in 1794. Colonel John's lawyer, Charles M'Intosh, handled the purchase of Wester Gask bordering the M'Gillivray's farm of Easter Gask.

Two years later, Campbell M'Intosh was dismayed when a member of the consortium tried to pull out of the Curatory: 'Mr. Inglis has had the chief trouble in the business hitherto and has declined to continue.' The other curators feared that no-one else equal to the task could be found to replace him. Of Barbara Ann in Greenwich, M'Intosh wrote, 'I hope there will be no objection to her remaining where she is until next midsummer - I do not wish it longer - she grows a fine girl and I trust her friends in the North will not think the money thrown away when they see her again.'

In America, Lachlan's son, Alexander, Chief of the Creek Nation, died in February 1993. After this, his son Aleck was sent to school in Banff, Scotland; this was paid for by his father's business associates, not his grandfather. Aleck was not mentioned in Lachlan's Deed of Settlement (there was no will or inventories).[56] Again, John Lachlan was the only heir, except for a very minor legatee, Marjory, Lachlan's niece who was living 'in family' with him in 1795.

If Lachlan's desire was to set up a strong and powerful M'Gillivray family in Scotland, he was not of the times: clans and chiefs were already of the past. While some, the M'Intoshes in particular, consolidated their position in the Highland capital, others left for London, North America, the West Indies, Australia or New Zealand, never to return. Inverness was losing its sons to the army,

---

[55] SC 29/10/1237 at National Archives of Scotland. Reverend Duncan Mackenzie's genealogy of the Dunmaglass family is held among the Murchison papers deposited at the University of Edinburgh.

[56] Aleck died two years after Lachlan.

the colonies or the attractions of the southern metropolis. Poorer and pious emigrants aspired to live in health and security, and strike it rich if possible. What wisdom did Lachlan retain, what lessons did he ponder in the farmstead of Dunmaglass, watching in his old age the sun rise and set over the Strathnairn moors? The greatest M'Gillivray of his time died on 16 November 1799, and his life remains a secret, buried in the past. No inventories were made, no will found in a repository. At death, the secret endured. Dunlichity graveyard is full of old gravestones, but there is no stone to mark Lachlan's grave. John Lachlan failed to erect a monument in memory of his august benefactor, of unknown relationship.

Lachlan's neighbour and relation Catherine Mackintosh of Farr, daughter of Alexander M'Gillivray of the Carolinas and Knocknagael, wrote to her son in India in November 1799: 'Our old friend Mr. Lachlan M'Gillivray died on the 16th instant, he had a very genteel burial, there were more gentlemen and carriages there than was ever seen in our parish churchyard.'

Soon afterwards, Captain William's daughter, Barbara Ann, said by Charles Fraser-Mackintosh to be a lady of great beauty, died in Edinburgh. We have only a series of sums of money to describe her last enigmatic days. She was attended by her maternal aunt, Marjory Mackenzie Walcot, who withdrew £75 between 24 May and 21 June 1800 for her niece's use, a large sum given her annual allowance of £50. On 15 June, her trustees made a first and tardive investment in her name with a £1000 loan to Cameron of Letterfinlay; these were the funds that had presumably been put aside for her by her uncle Colonel John and mentioned in her father's will. On 23 June, Barbara ordered two dozen bottles of red port and sherry, a sheep and a dozen hens and chickens to be shipped from Inverness, destination unknown, by the cutter Prince of Wales to one Simon Fraser, Esquire, at a total cost of £6.1.0d. On 27 August, this same or another Simon Fraser in Edinburgh, acting as procurator for the children's curators, gave a discharge to the former tutors. Barbara Ann died two days later. Obituaries were inserted in three Scottish newspapers. Her grave at Dunlichity bears the simple inscription: 'Sacred to the memory of Barbara Ann, only daughter of William M'Gillivray, Esq of Dunmaglass, who died on 29.06.1800 aged 19 years.'

The following month, Alexander of Knocknagael's widow, Anne Fraser, died at the age of 81 at Aldourie. Her financial circumstances had greatly improved for some unknown reason, coinciding with the Loyalists' arrival from America or with her son-in-law's succession to the Kyllachy estate. At the end of 1783, she had written to Provost John M'Intosh: 'I have received what may be thought a good deal of money in the past two years...' Sir James Mackintosh had just learnt his brother was murdered in the West Indies and now mourned the death of 'my most excellent grandmother', recalling her 'tender care of my infancy and youth'.

A year or two later, Miss Anne M'Gillivray, who had continued occupation of Aberchalder died. She named four heirs to her estate, which comprised the funds from the sale of the property: Alexander M'Gillivray in Daviot (son of Archibald), Donald M'Gillivray in Dalscoilt (father of William of the North West Company), Alexander M'Gillivray, coppersmith in Inverness (married to Jean Roy's daughter Marjory) and Lt. John and Mrs. Ann Fraser in Errogie.

Farquhar of Dalcrombie predeceased her. In 1793, for unknown reasons, he turned to Lachlan for £300, Provost Phineas M'Intosh and his cousin Provost William M'Intosh for £242, using his estate as security. There had been rioting that year in Inverness. When faced with grain shortages, the townspeople tried to prevent the magistrates from exporting grain to more lucrative markets; the latter accused the 'lower classes' of subversion that came from reading Thomas Paine. If Dalcrombie was still trading, he may have been affected. Three years later, Farquhar sold the lands that had been in his family for three generations, perhaps because none of his children wanted to live in Dalcrombie or to avoid favouring one child over another, for he treated them equally in his will. His eldest son William was in the army (71st Regiment) and would die at the farm of Dell, about Lachlan there is no information, John had left for Canada to work with his relation in the North West Company and Donald was farming at Drumboy.[57] Of his daughters, Janet was

---

[57] Farr says Donald died in the West Indies. William of Montreal left a legacy to his 'cousin' John; William's grandmother Mary M'Gillivray may well then have been of this Dalcrombie family. Farquhar of Dalcrombie's daughter Isabella was widowed in 1792 (she had a number of young children and her eldest son Simon was in Demerara at the

married to Michael M'Gillivray, now bulkmaster in Inverness, Isabella, whose eldest son was in Demerara, was widowed when Fraser died in 1792, and Johanna, who was born when her father was over sixty and presumably named after Dunmaglass' wife, would soon marry Alexander Dallas, saddler in Inverness.[58]

There was interest from several purchasers at a 'roup' or auction for the estate of Dalcrombie. Farquhar must have watched anxiously as four bidders had the turn of a half-hour glass to up their offers: David Davidson, one of the wealthiest men in Inverness, was the highest bidder at £3,200. He gave Farquhar and his son Lt. William a tack on a graceful new little manor house, farm and mill at Rosevalley, adjoining his property of Cantray. Farquhar spent his last years with a third wife Margaret Shaw of Tordarroch in idyllic peace on the banks of the river Nairn.

Feeling his end draw near, Farquhar pressed for settlement of his long overdue accounts with Colonel John's executors and the Dunmaglass estate. He had received neither his legacy from Colonel John nor his fees for the work on Gask. The sheriff depute of Inverness found he was owed a hefty £1,200. There remained one last duty to attend to. A tripartite debt was created when Aberchalder was purchased: of the price of the property, Farquhar owed Anne, its seller, £400; Colonel John owed Farquhar £400 and Anne owed either Colonel John or Farquhar £400. We do not know how Colonel John reimbursed Farquhar, but he allowed Anne to continue living in Aberchalder as long as she paid the interest on her debt, while Dalcrombie had to pay her the same amount to her. There was therefore an annual exchange of £20. Colonel John's executors knew of this debt and counter-debt. Now Farquhar gave

---

time), while daughter Janet was living in Inverness with her husband Michael and two children.

[58] Sadly Johanna wouldn't live long. She died in 1809 in the 26th year of her age. The most beautiful inscription in the whole of Chapel Yard cemetery is in her honour; it was composed by her stricken husband: 'Reader attend & if thine eye let fall a silent tear, confess it nature's call, consign'd to God from whence the blessing came, here lie the precious relicks of that frame, which whence inform'd with life attractive shin'd, with all we hope or wish of woman kind, adorn'd her manners in each sphere of life, the daughter, friend, the sister & the wife, this treasure lost what tongue can speake the smart, her mourning family feel & every kindred heart, but chiefly his whose sorrowful bosom prov'd, the lost endearments of his sole belov'd.'

Johanna and her husband £400 as a dowry, instructing them to pay the interest to Anne and on her demise to his third wife. As it was, Anne had only weeks to live.

Any evil that Farquhar of Dalcrombie did was not interred with his bones. One hundred years later, Charles Fraser-Mackintosh judged him the wickedest man in Inverness, together with John Macpherson in Ballachroan. There are instances where he appears dishonest and many others where he is harsh, but does he deserve such a severe epitaph? What could be said to redeem Dalcrombie, knowing that even Macpherson in Ballachroan had virtues and defenders? He was the poor guardian of his rich cousins' properties; he managed their estates efficiently albeit deviously. He seems to have treated his children equally. Still, this is laudable rather than virtuous so let us look at the context instead. The society he lived in had many who made hefty fortunes from the sweat and tears of slaves in the colonies; it gave positions of power to some who abusively took advantage to improve their personal fortunes. Fraser-Mackintosh's own relative, Provost Phineas, who improperly took land from the town of Inverness and was later censored by a Royal Commission, is a prime example. Dalcrombie's illicit still does not rank high on the ladder of abuses, although any slyness or trickery that was so successful that it escapes our notice might well.

Farquhar already had two monuments erected at Dunlichity, one on the death of his first wife in 1760, the second in 1767 to his then living second wife. But neither of these was inscribed with the place and date of his own burial by any dutiful heir.

Jean, the attributed daughter of the Captain Ban, lived well into the new century, presumably in Balnagaig, dying about the year 1810 'at a very advanced age'.

Wealth in the parish of Daviot and Dunlichity

According to the 1841 Statistical Account of the parish of Daviot and Dunlichity, the earliest parish registers were destroyed when the schoolhouse where they were kept burnt down. The 1791 Statistical Account reported that since 1788 no register of baptisms or marriages had been kept 'owing to an incident'. There is one surviving register (1774-1820) with irregular entries. In his report of the parish, Reverend MacPhail wrote that at Dunmaglass and Farr 'the improvement of draining, enclosing and planting has been for sometime carried on with propriety and success….The state of agriculture is in extreme backwardness.'

Small black oats and rye were the principal crops; common oats and barley would not grow. Rev. MacPhail criticised landlords for demanding services in lieu of money to rent the land, finding this practice detrimental to progress. About 2,000 blackfaced sheep had been introduced by 1840 and the number of cattle had declined as a consequence. There were 1,265 parishioners. This congregation was often joined by Episcopalians (430 in number) whose chapel only held a service once every three or four weeks.

The parishioners had a 'sense of shame and honour, in a high degree for their station. They are frugal; and they would be industrious if the climate and other particular circumstances offered the same excitement which happier situations possess. There are about 60 young men who migrate southwards for employment during the seasons of spring, summer and harvest: but by this means they have not generally increased their stock…'

He wrote that the people prepared peat and turf fuel, carried it to the markets of the town twice a week throughout the year. There were a considerable number of weavers employed in making coarse woolen fluff. Corn-mills also employed some local people.

He praised Colonel John and the M'Intoshes of Aberarder and Farr for planting the Scots fir. 'These gentlemen were first who attempted planting or any other improvement in the country (…) The external appearance of the country is not very inviting, and must seem rather wild and romantic to a stranger.'

It was difficult for many families to eke out a living due to the small size of their landholdings, infertile soil and an inclement climate. In fact, it is surprising that anybody, however frugal, could put aside money. Nevertheless, a number of these Gaelic-speaking crofters were willing to pay to register their wills. In 1800, at the time of Lachlan's death, a series of M'Gillivray wills were recorded in the deed book for Inverness. In 1800, Donald M'Gillivray, 'in good circumstances', foxhunter in nearby Strathdearn, was able to leave three sisters in Balnacarnish of Easter Aberchalder some

£30.[59] In 1807, again at Balnacarnish, Gaelic-speaking Janet M'Gillivray, wife of John M'Intosh, neither of whom could read or write, used a notary to dispose of her effects. In 1803, another Gaelic-speaking and illiterate tenant in Dalriach, John M'Gillivray, left a will and a small annuity to his daughter-in-law.

One M'Gillivray with means was Donald, a drover and cattle dealer also at Balnacarnish of Easter Aberchalder. But he drew bills that were not honoured and went bankrupt in 1821. His creditors were John M'Gillivray in Keppoch, William M'Gillivray in Balnacarnish, Farquhar M'Gillivray in Dalreach, and Duncan and Mary Macpherson in Keppoch. Any funds owing him were placed with Archibald McTavish in Garthbeg, Donald Roy's son in law. This Donald from Balnacarnish makes a totally unexpected and surprising reappearance at the end of this history.

The most astonishing deed for the sum and generosity was by William M'Gillivray, a Gaelic-speaking tenant in Ballanortan of Aberchalder in the 1830s. He mortified £400 sterling; one quarter of the interest for the poor of Aberchalder and three quarters for those of Dunlichity. Although the sum was small in comparison with the £10,000 left by Simon Fraser Mackintosh of Farr's uncle, Captain William of the Hindustan Indiaman, for the education of poor M'Intosh boys, it is an astonishing amount from someone who 'cannot write for never having been taught' as he records. William assigned the funds to John Lachlan of Dunmaglass and other neighbours for his legacies.[60]

It was difficult to accrue wealth from the infertile soils or keeping sheep, and the source of his funds is unknown. Perhaps the wealthy Colonel John, Lachlan, Farquhar of Dalcrombie or William of the North West Company made unrecorded bequests to these people who were mostly from Aberchalder.

Towards the end of the 18th century, another M'Gillivray family living in this parish was in fortunate circumstances. In the mid-

---

[59] This seems to be Donald M'Gillivray, whose bill was allegedly forged by John Grant, sheriff-clerk depute of Inverness. Grant was accused of forgery and transported to Australia; the magistrates of Inverness were uncomfortable that 'one of theirs' was found guilty of dishonesty.

[60] When William of Dundee still hadn't received his legacy in 1839, he took the trustees to court.

1700s, Alexander (Borlum) M'Intosh of Raigmore lived at the farm of Croachy in Dunmaglass, while his daughter Jean and her husband Lachlan M'Intosh lived at the Mains of Aberarder. Alexander at Croachy and his son-in-law at Aberarder were involved in the doings of the notorious Edward M'Intosh, the last laird of Borlum, who has gone down in history as a highway robber who fled for his life to France. His brother Alastair was hanged at Muirfield, still protesting his innocence and believed by many, but not the judge. Alexander at Croachy and his son-in-law were put in Inverness Tolbooth for spiriting away certain witnesses who could have testified against Edward. The two men were released in May 1773 when Provost Phineas M'Intosh acted as cautioner.

When Lachlan in Aberarder died, his widow Jean remarried a Duncan M'Gillivray, lived in Tullich and had at least four more children, Donald, Jean, Janet and Margaret born after 1776.[61] Later, Jean moved to Inverness. Her brother William returned from India with a considerable fortune and bought Geddes House near Cawdor. He had no children and the property was inherited by Jean's sons Alexander and William, who both worked for the East India Company. William, styled Dr. M'Intosh from his years in the medical service in India, 'kept up a large establishment', and a rebuilt Geddes House became a centre of great hospitality and festivity. William of Geddes then had a M'Gillivray half-brother and sisters but we cannot trace what became of them.

---

[61] A. Mackintosh Shaw

CHAPTER FIVE
JOHN LACHLAN AND HIS HEIRS

19th century clan chief

Of John Lachlan's life we know little. He lived with Lachlan and his aunt Anne. He played backgammon as a child, was a difficult charge for his tutors, and enrolled at St. Andrew's at the age of fourteen. He bought a cornetcy in the 16th Light Dragoons when he was eighteen and served in Ireland during the rebellion. He left the army young and married his older step-cousin Jane Walcot ('a lady who had much influence with him for good' according to Charles Fraser Mackintosh) in August 1805 when he was twenty-three. At the time, Inverness society frequently intermarried: Jane's father, a widower, had earlier married John Lachlan's Mackenzie aunt. The couple had no children but much money. By 1803, the rental of the estates was bringing him in £544 from 71 tenants. John Lachlan had also inherited funds and bonds from his uncle John and his relation Lachlan. Despite this wealth and good fortune, Catherine Mackintosh of Farr, daughter of Alexander M'Gillivray of the Carolinas and Knocknagael, refers to him in her correspondence as 'poor M'Gillivray' or 'M'Gillivray poor fellow', as though somehow he was to be pitied.

The MacGillivray Clan book notes that he was a skilled swordsman and, on one occasion, was challenged to a duel by young Forbes of Culloden. He accepted but first asked Forbes to help him fetch over a rainwater barrel, into which, he told an electrified Forbes, he intended to 'place his carved out innards'.

The M'Gillivrays did not live in Dunmaglass but in the mansion at Drummond, rented from Provost Phineas M'Intosh.

When Phineas entailed his estate in a complicated package to his nephew M'Intosh of Holm, John Lachlan, a second cousin of Holm's, was first in the list of trustees, although he declined to continue in this office when Phineas died in 1812. John Lachlan would have found himself among his peers and relations, the Inverness notables at the beginning of the 19th century: Simon

Fraser, Esq. of Farraline, John Fraser, advocate, younger of Farraline, George Inglis, Esq. of Kingsmills, Archibald and William Alves, Esqs. sons of the deceased Dr John Alves, physician in Inverness, William Baillie, Esq. of Dunain, John M'Intosh, Esq. of Aberarder, William M'Intosh, younger of Aberarder, Lachlan M'Intosh, Esq. of Raigmore and William M'Intosh, Esq. of Geddes. In 1815 John Lachlan became a director of the Inverness Parish or Savings Bank, a project run by the Inverness Farmers' Society. Fellow directors included Sheriff Fraser-Tytler, Inglis of Kingsmills, Peter Anderson, solicitor, and Messrs. M'Intosh of Holm, Raigmore and Kinmylies.

But John Lachlan delighted more in hunting, shooting and riding. From Drummond, he corresponded with his cousin Barbara Mackenzie's son, Kenneth Murchison, about all manner of hunting and in return was sent baskets of pheasants from London and the latest court gossip. When Barbara married Colonel Robert M'Gregor Murray, John Lachlan went to stay with them near Durham and sent urgently to Inverness for more money; he led the life of a Highland laird and apparently showed no interest in his more modest paternal relations, the Roses, Frasers, Pattisons and Davidsons.

He also travelled abroad 'a great deal' according to Charles Fraser-Mackintosh. They appear in Marseille and Naples in 1820 but we do not know where else he and his wife traveled. Many of their contemporaries left diaries of their travels and thoughts, but if John Lachlan wrote, nothing has survived.

The Highlanders were continuing their exodus to North America in great numbers, forced off their lands or in search of better prospects abroad. Dunmaglass and the other estates were affected. In 1803, John Lachlan had 71 tenants. By 1819, the numbers were down to 59; at his death in 1852, there were less than half that number. In 1816 and 1817, he placed advertisements in the Inverness Journal for the rental of Dunmaglass, Gask, Faillie and Invererny, and again in 1829 for the rental of Dunmaglass, Balnagaig and Dalscoilt. Any responsibility or grand design for the members of his clan, whose lands were now his, was inexistent: John Lachlan, like many of the other clan chiefs, had become an absentee landlord. The lands that were once a livelihood for his clansmen became shooting grounds for the privileged or pastureland for sheep.

It was reported to the later Napier Commission that thirteen farmers were turned off Dunmaglass and Aberchalder in 1839-40 and the cleared land turned into a large sheep and deer farm. John Lachlan then lived at Margaret Street leading off Academy Street, lodging with the Clarks who were fellow-members of the Episcopal congregation of Inverness. Their daughter Charlotte was his (fortunate) housekeeper. Despite his wealth, he never bought a house in town, nor went to live in Dunmaglass.

The description we have of John Lachlan from Charles Fraser-Mackintosh, from his own choice of women to look after him, from his life of idleness, from Catherine Mackintosh of Farr's epithet of 'poor fellow' up to his child-like final wishes, hints that the 'infant gentleman' may have turned into something of a simpleton. Fraser-Mackintosh noted that after his wife's death in 1843, Dunmaglass led a somewhat retired life 'and many will recollect his fine military carriage, and how well he sat on horseback as he took his daily rides in Inverness'.

Fraser-Mackintosh added: 'When he was in his cups, he would say he was descended of kings.' If this referred to the kings of Scotland, it is unworthy of repetition; if not another hint of feeble-mindedness, we could here see a reference to the Roy M'Gillivrays, whom we shall see later.

We see from the genealogies drawn up by his Episcopal minister, Duncan Mackenzie, that Dunmaglass never spoke of his roots, of his early mentor, Lachlan from Georgia, or of Jean who may or may not have looked after him in his childhood.

John Lachlan died on 6 February 1852 and was buried a week later at Dunlichity. The cortège consisted of four mourning coaches, each drawn by four horses, and a large number of 2-horse carriages, gigs and equestrians. The Laird of M'Intosh did not attend. A farcical incident lightened the proceedings: on one of the coaches, Macdonald, the lawyers' clerk, fell asleep on the box of a coach, toppled off and was run over. He broke his leg above the knee and was taken back to Inverness and a doctor. Apparently, he had been drinking. John Lachlan was buried next to his wife Jane Walcot, and the marble reads:

'Sacred to the memory of Jane Walcot, the beloved and lamented wife of John Lachlan M'Gillivray, Esq of Dunmaglass, who died at Edinburgh on 10.10.1843. Her life was eminently distinguished by the exercise of the Christian virtues and she died in the fulness of a Christian faith and hope. This ornamental stone is placed on her remains in affectionate and sorrowing remembrance by her attached and devoted husband and to the memory of John Lachlan M'Gillivray, Esq of Dunmaglass, chief of the clan M'Gillivray, who died at Inverness on 06.02.1852. The full scope of blessed immortality, the dignity of his deportment, the strength of his attachment and his unrestrained liberality of the poor will long be remembered. Blessed are they (that) considereth the poor, the Lord Knoweth them are his.'

John Lachlan's will

The local notables were agog with curiosity about the will, but it was a restricted group that assembled that evening for the reading by the trustees and executors, Mr. Belfond, banker and Dr. Walker, physician. The small group was composed of John Lachlan's accountants, his spiritual mentors and one or two trusted friends. Patrick Grant, sheriff-clerk of Inverness and future judicial factor of the Dunmaglass estates, Charles Robertson, accountant, George Anderson, probably of the Inverness Bank, banker Waterston, Reverends Duncan Mackenzie of Tullich and James Mackay of Stoneyfield, a Mr. M'Gillivray from Fort William and Miss Charlotte Clark, housekeeper.

The odd-man-out who remains unidentifiable is Mr. M'Gillivray from Fort William. As we have seen, John Lachlan had no M'Gillivray first cousins and no male second cousins apart from one Dalcrombie in Canada. A formal right or reason for this Mr. M'Gillivray to be in the assembly existed, but we do not know what it was. He was neither a legatee nor a witness to the will. The census of 1851 of Fort William shows only one male M'Gillivray: twenty-one year old John, a general storekeeper, son of Benjamin M'Gillivray of the 92nd Regiment, who was born in Boleskine in 1777 of John and Isobel Macpherson.

The assembly must have been as astonished by the will as others were later. The principal heir was his housekeeper, Charlotte Clark 'in consideration of her services to my late wife and myself'. Charlotte's legacy was £6,000 (her two sisters Catherine and Christian received lesser amounts), Dr. Walker and daughters £1,400, and £1000 each to Mrs. Fyvie (widow of the Episcopal Minister of Inverness), her sister Mrs. McLauchlin, Charles Robertson, Esquire, Mr. Sullivan and several members of his wife's Walcot family. They were also his residuary legatees, so that the sums would be at least tripled, if not quadrupled, according to Rev. Mackay who must have had this estimation from good source.

Numerous legacies went to well-heeled maternal relations: General Sir Alexander Mackenzie, last of Fairburn (his cousin) and the children of cousin Barbara Mackenzie whose first husband, Kenneth Murchison, had acquired his Tarradale estate with the fortune he made curing the Nabob of Arcot's daughter of distemper. John Lachlan bequeathed legacies to their son, Sir Roderick Impey Murchison, and to the two sons of his brother Kenneth, John Lachlan's hunting partner. Sir Roderick in later years became an eminent self-taught scientist, chairman of the Geological Society, while his brother Kenneth was governor of Singapore. The son of one of their half-sisters, Barbara M'Gregor Murray, was also remembered.

Other bequests went to distant members of his wife Jane Walcot's family, to the Episcopal chapel of Strathnairn to build a new school, purchase a communion plate and feed the poor, to the needy in the congregation of the Episcopal Chapel of Inverness, to the Reverends McKenzie and Mackay and to John Lachlan's two servants. The most welcomed of the bequests was one year's rent, representing over £1,500, to all the tenants. The most unexpected was to John Charles William Paul Graham of Drynie.

John Charles, scarcely ten years of age, was the orphaned son of George Graham of Drynie and his partner Anne Pauline Camille de Calvy de St. André. He was born in Paris, France, and baptised by the chaplain at the British Embassy. His birth occurred in the middle of much litigation, as he was heir to a great fortune. His guardians were George W. F. Villiers, Earl of Clarendon and Secretary of State for Foreign Affairs, and Sir Roderick Impey

Murchison. The appointment of Sir Roderick, Barbara Mackenzie's son, as guardian suggests that this Graham family of Drynie was of the Grahams of Charleston, and seemingly the family into which John Lachlan's maternal relation Isobel Mackenzie had married. Graham had handled Lachlan's business affairs and witnessed the marriage of John Lachlan's parents.

Had George Graham died without issue, distant cousins would have inherited the entailed estates. Robert Gordon Munro, one time of Jamaica, had grown accustomed to the idea of one day inheriting the Graham fortune and entered into fruitless negotiations with his childless Graham relation in France. When the latter wrote that he would soon be the father of a child, a disbelieving Munro went to the courts. Camille miscarried and, for every subsequent pregnancy, she was obliged by court order to submit to examinations carried out by doctors attached to the British Embassy. Each time they were unable to ascertain that she was pregnant. When sixty-two year old Graham announced through his solicitors the arrival of a son without one of these standard medical checks, Munro claimed that any child of George Graham in general, and this child, John Charles William Paul, in particular, was a fraud and impostor. He claimed that George and Camille were not married, that they had lived together for thirty-two years without producing a child and that, in any case, Camille had left Graham and was living with another English gentleman in Paris. Although Munro's litigation was in vain as the child was declared heir (and eventually sold the estates), Graham genealogists state that in his putative father, George Graham, 'the male line virtually ended'.

The child was already wealthy. His inclusion in the will indicates not so much that John Lachlan desired to improve the child's fortune but that he felt an attachment or sympathy for the child. Had John Lachlan's own birth aroused similar suspicions?

When the reading of John Lachlan's will was over, Rev. James Mackay returned to Stoneyfield and wrote post-haste to the M'Intosh chief at Moy who was expecting a report. If Mackay was astonished at some of the bequests in the will, he kept his feelings to himself. 'It is my particular wish that my remains shall be enterred at Dunlichity at the foot of those of my wife and also that the said Charlotte Clark's remains may be interred in same ground.'

Victorian lawyers, staring at him through their pince-nez from behind mahogany desks, would have been shocked: his housekeeper was not only his principal heir, John Lachlan declared, but also to be buried beside him.[62]

Later accounts and inventories drawn up by the solicitors valued John Lachlan's estate at £29,460.4.9 1/2d. This is less than Rev. Mackay had in mind when he estimated that the residuary heirs would treble or quadruple their legacies. Apparently, John Lachlan's fortune was smaller than his neighbours thought. It is curious that they were wide off the mark: perhaps John Lachlan had given away many of his assets beforehand, or he lived above his means and made bad investments.

He had left legacies to a number of distant relatives on his mother's side who, as we have seen, were in no need of material assistance, to relatives of his deceased wife in southern England, to his housekeeper and her sisters, and to no-one of the name M'Gillivray, nor anyone with a M'Gillivray mother. This noticeable absence must confirm the accepted genealogies: he had no M'Gillivray relatives. Neither did he name an heir to his estate of Dunmaglass – he turned this over to the courts and lawyers to decide. But what is astounding is that although he himself had been richly favoured by a cousin of his father's, he made no similar bequest to this man's family. They were more closely related than the Mackenzie or Walcot beneficiaries and their circumstances were not as fortunate. Why did be believe he owed them nothing? One possible conclusion is that he did not want anyone to know who these relatives were, another is that they were not his kin.

There was no benefit for any M'Gillivray in particular, but those who were tenants, however few, were well recompensed. Each was summoned by the executors and given a sum equal to one year's rent of their farms. When Archibald Thomas Frederick Fraser, Esquire of Abertarff and Colonel Henry Cracklan of the HEIC, both great sportsmen, demanded to know why they were not summoned, the executors pointed out with some indignation that

---

[62] Although we are unable to link Charlotte Clark's father John from Petty with the Daniel Clark who shared the farm of Dalzeil with the Dalcrombies and later worked with Lachlan in America in the early 18th century, there may be a connection. Was she a distant relative?

John Lachlan had not intended the opulent holders of shooting rights to benefit. The two gentlemen turned to the courts for their opinion and won: they too received their legacy of one year's shooting dues.

Uncertainty

On 17 February 1852, *The Inverness Advertiser* published this report:

'The heir apparent of the estate of Dunmaglass, in Strathnairn, at the rebellion of 1745, was Robert or Rorie More, as he was commonly called, who gallantly headed the Clan M'Intosh at the battle of Culloden on the 16th April 1746, and fell there in the desperate attack on the English lines, along with several gentlemen of his family and many of their retainers. The late John Lachlan M'Gillivray, whose death is recorded in our paper of to-day, had a warm affection for his clan, and shewed it by ordering in his will a year's rent to be remitted to all the tenants on his estates - a most seasonable boon, we dare say, to many of them. He also left several bequests to parties in and about Inverness, and some charitable donations, and liberally contributed to the funds of the Episcopal congregations in Strathnairn and Inverness, with which he and his forefathers were connected.

It is understood that the heir to the estate will be any member of the family of M'Gillivray in Ballintruan, if any such exist. The last known head of that family was a gun-maker or armourer in Edinburgh, who is believed to have removed latterly (about 50 years ago) to Liverpool, and to have left a son of whom no accounts have been heard for a long time. Failing that family the M'Gillivrays of Dalcrombie succeed, and they are at present represented by the Hon. John M'Gillivray of Montreal, Canada, who, it is understood, some time ago, instructed an agent in Scotland to look after his interest in the event of the demise of the late Dunmaglass.'

The Inverness Advertiser made a curious mistake about the head of the M'Gillivrays at the time of Culloden. Initially, Robert was believed to be the Dunmaglass of the mid-18th century, or perhaps the newspaper's source was Rev. Duncan Mackenzie who claimed his wife's ancestor to be commander of the M'Intosh force. The mistake was continued by George Bain in *The Lordship of Petty* and later writers. Alexander was Dunmaglass and his heir apparent was a younger brother, or if none existed, a son of the Captain Ban. Curiously, *The Inverness Advertiser* passes over his existence completely.

The report nevertheless shows the early odds were on Dunmaglass going to the Canadian branch if there was no male issue of younger brother David. In this they were right. But they were wrong to presume that he would succeed to the whole of John Lachlan's estate.

The Ballintruan[63] cousins

David, younger brother of Farquhar and the Captain Ban, and his wife at Mid-Leys had transferred the wadset or lease of their farm to their Dunmaglass nephew and it was thus forfeited in 1747 as one of his possessions. Somehow the estate returned to the original family; their son Alexander sold it in the early 1750s and by 1767 had taken on the tack of Lairgs, or Lairgantruan. By 1794, he had moved to Balindrynan, a croft at Faillie, where Isabelle Fraser, widow of 'Big John of the Markets' had been an earlier tenant. The proceeds from Mid-Leys did not apparently improve his circumstances for, according to the letter from William to Lachlan, he was too poor to educate the children of a 'mean' marriage.

Alexander's son John received a legacy in Colonel John's will, and with money advanced by Lachlan, equipped himself to go abroad as an army ensign, and disappeared. Colonel John with some ill-determined intention or irony left second son David 'two good field slaves, one male and one female'. David reportedly became an armourer or coppersmith in Edinburgh. Neither of the sons presented a claim for Dunmaglass, and nothing further is known about them.

---

[63] Sometimes rendered as 'Balindrynan'

Although the sons vanished, the four daughters all married local farmers. Their descendants could not of course inherit Dunmaglass for the feu charter from the Thanes of Cawdor destined it to heirs-male. These descendants though were well-placed to inherit the lands that were not entailed.

Eldest daughter Catherine (1756-1804) married William, son of Duncan Rose, co-tacksman with her father in Lairgantur, lands where the Jacobite M'Gillivrays assembled before the battle of Culloden.[64] Their eldest son Duncan, a claimant, was born in 1785, married Ann M'Bean and farmed at Bridgend of Tomatin, where he died in 1865.

Second daughter Margaret married Alexander Fraser, principal tenant of the farm in Mid-Faillie, once occupied by Michael, Dalcrombie's son-in-law. These were the lands bought by William or Lachlan in the 1770s. Alexander Fraser in Mid-Faillie was baillie in March 1792 for John Lachlan's infeftment. As was the common form, Fraser 'gave and delivered heritable state and sasine, actual, real and corporal possession of all and whole (the said lands) to John Lachlan M'Gillivray, delivering in the hands of the said William M'Bean as procurator foresaid, of earth and stone of and upon the ground of the said lands respectively, clapp and happer of the said mill, and all other symbols usual and requisite after the form and tenor of the said precept of sasine'.

Two years later Fraser witnessed a deed drawn up by Lachlan giving John, his wife's young brother, an advance of Colonel John's inheritance. Thomas Fraser, his eldest son, born circa 1777, joined the North West Company when William M'Gillivray was rising in power and importance, and called his Canadian home Faillie in memory of the Scottish farm. As chief trader at Abitibi and Timiskaming, Thomas was noted for his thrift and described as 'a strong, hardy fellow who can live where an Indian would starve'. When the company collapsed, he joined the Hudson's Bay Company and he and wife Flora McTavish, daughter of John George McTavish, Dunardry's son, by his métisse wife Nancy McKenzie, named their son George Simpson Fraser after the

---

[64] Relationships in this family appear in inscriptions on gravestones, particularly the stone erected by Fraser McIntosh Rose, OBE.

president of the company, a close friend. Thomas died in 1849, leaving an 11-year-old son, George, and a daughter, Frances. When young George declared himself a claimant for the M'Gillivray lands, he was studying medicine at Lennoxville College in the County of Sherbroke. He later joined the army and served in India.

Third daughter Ann married Lachlan Paterson in March 1781. Anne at Dunmaglass gave her young namesake a tocher or dowry eight years later. The couple lived at Kessock, across the Moray Firth from Inverness, and had sons Lachlan and William. William's son Donald was the claimant - his elder brother having recently died without legitimate issue - and was a salmon fisher in Berriedale, in the county of Caithness.

Youngest daughter was Amelia or Millicent (1771-1817), undoubtedly the newborn infant that Bishop Forbes' Journal indicates was carried many miles to be baptised by Episcopal rite. Coincidentally, Amelia's husband was also named Alexander Fraser and they lived with her father at Ballintruan with several children: John, Lachlan, Jannet and Catherine. Eldest son, John, merchant in Newcastle-upon-Tyne in England, represented this family in the claim.

This then was the Ballintruan family that stood to gain if there was no nearer heir to their second cousin; their genealogy seemed clear and proof of descent was available. The 1727 baptism of David's son Alexander was registered in the parish register of Dores, although registers for baptisms for the following generations do not survive. Weight would be added to their claim if the four men stood as a block corroborating each other's descent; this they were ready to do. Their mandatory was Donald M'Bean, also from Ballintruan.

Next-of-kin

The second court-case, which proceeded as slowly as the first in the Edinburgh courts only with a startling interruption that dragged it out even longer, concerned the lands that Lachlan probably bought during his two-year visit to Scotland from 1770. These were not entailed to a male heir and would be awarded to the descendants, male or female, of the next younger brother of Farquhar born circa 1680: William or David. Neil John, now in possession of Dunmaglass and Aberchalder, argued that the lands of Faillie were restricted by their deeds to an owner who was member of the Clan Chattan, so he sought entitlement as next-of-kin with a Clan Chattan name, and as descending from William and David's sister Janet.

David's descendants pulled out some years into the litigation, either because they judged they could not dislodge the Captain Ban from his position of next younger brother, or because the litigation was proving too costly. Despite the initial silence concerning descendants of the Captain Ban, there were now more than enough. But they did not agree among themselves and participated in the claim as competitors.

Lucy

John M'Intosh or Davidson claimed he was the only surviving child of the deceased Donald Davidson, sometime forester to the Earl of Moray at Darnaway Castle[65] near Nairn, and of Janet Davidson, his wife, who was the only child of Captain Davidson, officer in the army and of his wife Lucy, daughter of the Captain Ban. Jean's descendants claimed that Jean was the only one of the Captain Ban's children who left issue, and denied their grandmother had a sister named Lucy.

The parish records confirm that Thomas Davidson married Lucia M'Giliwray (sic) in Inverness in 1744, that a Janet Davidson of Nairn married Donald Davidson of Edinkilly in 1770, and that the latter had at least four children: Francis, William, John and Janet (between 1775 and 1790). None of the godparents is a M'Gillivray (nor do these godparents appear to have a M'Gillivray mother). These are the Captain Ban's only identifiable great-grandchildren, but perhaps Dunmaglass was too far for family to attend or there were no more M'Gillivray relations left. Lachlan from America, the children's grand-uncle, was now in Scotland, and these were – if he was son of the Captain Ban – his closest relations apart from his

---

[65] At this period Darnaway was undergoing a vast reforestation programme with tens of millions of trees planted.

Creek grandson at Banff as of 1795 whom he seems to have ignored. Of approximately the same age as John Lachlan, these Davidson children, together with the Dalcrombie M'Gillivrays (through their female ancestor), and the descendants of David, were young Dunmaglass' closest kin on his father's side.

Under the name of M'Intosh and not Davidson, young John headed south to seek his fortune.[66] He joined the Dumfries militia and was stationed in Dalkeith where he married Elizabeth McLain; their children were named Frances Agnes, George Laidlaw Davidson, John, Jessie and William. John left the militia and worked as a bookbinder, bookseller and stationer in town. Daughter Frances married into a local Adamson family and had a child, John. Son George worked with his father and then moved to Kirkcaldy. After a few years, he removed to the 'large and commodious shop at the Public Buildings' where he opened 'a sales room, where furniture and shop good of all kinds will be taken in to be disposed of'. There were monthly auction sales of furniture and stationery. His father and younger sister joined him from Dalkeith; Jessie married locally (to James Morton) and in 1851, George married Janet Johnstone.

When John Lachlan's succession opened, John M'Intosh the bookseller drew up his genealogy, submitted it to the Sheriff Office, and then withdrew it to correct an unknown error. But before the litigation could proceed much further, he died at the end of 1856 'of general decay'. His death certificate states that his parents were Donald Davidson and Janet, maiden name Davidson. In the litigation, John is constantly referred to as Davidson. Neil John, who held that the successful claimant should be of Clan Chattan, denounced him for only recently taking the name M'Intosh, but as Davidson is as worthy a name as M'Intosh in the clan, it was a pointless accusation. It was also untrue, as George's baptismal entry at the beginning of the 18th century shows. But the legal system and the other claimants insisted on referring to him as Davidson. John's claim was taken up by his son George Laidlaw Davidson M'Intosh,

---

[66] The reasons for the name change are unknown. His godfather was John M'Intosh in Darnaway; perhaps as many another Highlander without issue, he had made the young man his heir on condition that he should adopt his name; Charles Fraser-Mackintosh, who took a maternal uncle's name, is another example of this display of respect for a benefactor. This John M'Intosh may have been a Kyllachy relation.

who pursued his claim and held to his descent with great vigour and determination.

Of significance is that in the litigation for Dunmaglass, Lachlan M'Intosh, who was cited by Neil John to confirm there were no closer male heirs than him, was agent for both the Ballintruan cousins and Lucy's descendants. We can conclude from this that there was no animosity between these parties. This was probably not the case as regards the descendants of Jean Roy. We should also note here that it was Reverend Lachlan who had introduced Jean as a sister to Lachlan, Indian trader, with the printed will he had presented at the first courtcase.

Jean Roy

According to the court proceedings, Lachlan's attributed sister, Jean, had three daughters by her marriage to Duncan Roy M'Gillivray in Balnagaig. Although two sons are mentioned in Lachlan and Colonel John's 1767 typewritten wills, there is no further reference to them. The daughters were: Janet born by 1757, Mary born 1767, and Marjory born later. The main tenant of this farm was Duncan's father William (see below). Jean's daughter Janet married John Macarthur in Mid-Fleenas in Ardclach (the following year they moved to Achneim in Cawdor), with a marriage contract drawn up by Farquhar of Dalcrombie in 1784.[67] John and Janet's daughter, Ann, widow of Francis Souter, writer and Excise Officer in Islay, was now a claimant. She was seventy and had a will of iron that was much respected or feared by those who knew her. Before marrying, her daughter Hamilton had lived with her paternal cousin, the Mrs. Brodie at Lethen House in Auldearn, near Nairn. The Brodies were highly respected members of Scotland's gentry, leading figures in freemasonry and the law. John Clerk Brodie, Esquire of Idvies, was Deputy Keeper of the Signet and Keeper of the General Register of Sasines for Scotland; his son Thomas, a

---

[67] There are no marriage contracts for her sisters. Janet signed her name 'Jenny' and is described as daughter of Duncan in Dunmaglass.

writer to the Signet.[68] Ann was therefore a well-connected claimant with the most powerful support in the country with relations from whom no secrets were hid, either in the form of family trusts or relationships.

The second sister, Marjory (presumably the Marjory mentioned by Lachlan in his Deed of Settlement as living 'in family' with him), had married Alexander M'Gillivray, a much-respected Inverness coppersmith and active freemason of unknown parentage. There were no children. The third sister, Mary, married Donald Noble, and it was their son, John M'Gillivray Noble, an upholsterer in London who was Ann's co-claimant; John Noble's sisters did not participate in the claim.[69] Intestate succession, even through the female line, still favoured males to females in the same degree of relationship, so Noble's sisters would have had no expectations.

The maternal genealogy of these claimants is uncertain as we do not know whose daughter Jean was. The paternal line seems clearer, thanks to William M'Gillivray of the North West Company of Canada. William's father Donald, married to Ann, sister of Simon McTavish, at one time the wealthiest man in Canada, had on occasion acted as procurator for Lachlan, and was clearly a local worthy, and latterly commanded the title 'Mr.' before his name in the parish register. Young William joined his McTavish uncle in Canada, took over when he died, and rivalled him in influence and wealth. When he returned to Scotland on his honeymoon in 1801, he applied for a grant of arms from the Lord Lyon. His uncle Simon had quite irregularly copied his chieftain's arms, and later purchased Dunardry, thereby stepping into the chieftain's place completely,

---

[68] Deputy Keeper of the Signet: the effective head of the Society of Writers to the Signet. All summonses in the Court of Session originally needed to go through the hands of the clerks in the royal secretariat of state which controlled the king's personal seal or signet. Warrants for service of summonses, and charges to implement the court's decrees, were required to be sealed with the signet. Keeper of the Registers: officer responsible for the Department of the Registers in which are maintained the General Register of Sasines, the Land Register of Scotland, and registers of a wide range of deeds relating to succession, trusts, family agreements and state appointments.

[69] Among John's sisters were Mary (married to William Tolmie, tailor in Nairn), May and Betsy (married to Alexander McKie, overseer in Applecross), who were named in their aunt Marjory's will; she did not mention John or her sister Janet's daughters. Also noted in her effects were silver spoons to go to one William M'Gillivray of the unrecognizable farm of 'Straaltown'.

which in the early 19th century was unacceptable. Nobody knew the arms of Dunmaglass, so William designed his own from scratch. He used the Campbell of Cawdor motto 'Be Mindful', a more refined rendering of clan Chattan's rabble-rousing 'Touch not the cat bot a glove'. The arms are said to resemble the Macphersons', which has given rise to some speculation about who in fact the clan followed, the M'Intoshes or the Macphersons.

The Lord Lyon King of Arms, the Earl of Kinnoull, describing the applicant as 'a virtuous and well deserving person', copied down his pedigree; his father was Donald (born in 1741, cf. gravestone; second name Roy cf. Dores parish register), son of William, son of Benjamin whose father was Farquhar, a younger son of the family of Dunmaglass.

Donald's parents were in 1746 tenants of Balnagaig, the largest farm of the Dunmaglass estate, paying the highest rent. Donald Roy and his brother Duncan are mentioned in the 1762 roup when Alexander Fraser, Lord Lovat's son, died at Dunmaglass. Their father William in Balnagaig had granted a bond in 1743 (perhaps post-nuptial if a son Duncan was already married by 1757) which was discharged in 1751, witnessed by Alexander of Knocknagael and Farquhar of Dalcrombie, giving his wife Mary M'Gillivray life rent over the town of Balnagaig. Given the two witnesses, Mary was clearly a member of the family in Lonnie or in Dalzeil.[70]

This William, then, was son of Benjamin, son of Farquhar, a younger son of the Dunmaglass family. It is unclear where this Farquhar fits in and whose son he was. If the epithet 'younger son' applies to Benjamin and not Farquhar, this could have been the son of Farquhar McAllister born in the late 17th century. There is no mention of any Benjamin, brother to Farquhar, the Captain Ban, Donald and David. Perhaps the family descended not from the 17th century Dunmaglass M'Gillivrays but from a Roy M'Gillivray who lived here at the time.[71] The Lyon Office in the early 19th century

---

[70] A Mary in 1747 married Thomas Fraser of Farraline. The parish register of Dores describes her as daughter of Dalcrombie but it is unclear which Dalcrombie family this is, so the parentage of both Marys (if it is not the same one) is uncertain. William in Balnagaig is mentioned in the will of Alexander in Lonnie in 1746.

[71] Lands of Dunmaglass in feu charter; 26 April 1626; one of witnesses was John Roy in Dunmaglass

granted arms without requiring much documentary support. The name Roy ('red') may originally have sprung from the colour of the hair, but by the 18th century, the Roy M'Gillivrays were a distinct family, the name appearing in deeds and parish registers where one would not expect to find commonplace nicknames.

There is scant information about these Roys: in 1778, Duncan was in disfavour with Dunmaglass' sister Anne for taking legal action to remove John M'Gillivray, an overseer appointed by Lachlan, from his quarter lands of Balnagaig. The following year, Dunmaglass in London instructed Dalcrombie to give Duncan Roy funds for the 'relief of education' of his children, the eldest being already in their twenties. Duncan had died or disappeared by 1781 when Jean was married to a John Mor M'Gillivray, perhaps the Balnagaig tenant her late husband had tried to remove. Jean died about 1810 at a 'very advanced' age. Her granddaughter Ann Macarthur Souter, one of the claimants, was already a young mother and of an age to remember her elderly grandmother. Jean's child-bearing years were between the mid 1750s and late 60s, so she was born between 1724 and 1734. She was certainly very young, perhaps an infant, when Lachlan left Scotland around 1735.

Jean's daughters

Jean's ancestry is problematic, and so is that of her grand-daughter Ann, as the proof the latter would have produced at the litigation is awkward. The parish registers have been added to or docked; it is difficult to verify the information, raising doubts about the ancestry claimed or hinting at an attempt to thwart Ann's entitlement. First of all, there is no marriage entry for John Macarthur and Janet M'Gillivray in the badly-kept parish register for Daviot & Dunlichity where she lived, nor in Ardclach where they settled once married. At the same time, in the neighbouring parish of Cawdor, the pages listing marriages between 1779 and 1793 have been torn from a well-kept register in a single act of vandalism on its pages. As John Macarthur and his wife were in Cawdor by 1790, it is possible they married here. Would their parishes of origin have confirmed or disproved what was submitted to the court?

Ann Souter stated that she was born in the summer of 1786 at the farm of Mid-Fleenas in Ardclach. A baptism record in the parish register has been added at the bottom of a page in different handwriting, probably at a later date to prove her descent for the litigation. The page on which it appears is the only one in the register that has been well-handled, torn and subsequently taped.

According to Ann, her mother Janet died on or about 25 March 1837 in Nairn when she was 'upwards of 80 years old'. The parish records of neighbouring Auldearn carry an early deaths register that includes Nairn. Again, only the page covering March 1837 when Janet died is missing in a second act of sabotage, and Janet's death record is lost. A ripped-out page could not have been presented as evidence at court; clerks had to make true and exact copies. It would again appear that a page had disappeared so that it would be difficult to either prove or disprove Janet's identity and place of death.

Janet's daughter Ann married Francis Souter, a 'riding' or excise officer, in Inverness on 11 July 1807. The marriage is entered in the Inverness registers regularly, but in the Cawdor register it has been inserted at a later date. The entry records what Ann testified in court, that she lived at Achneim in 1807 when she married. Family correspondence though shows that an unrelated family of Macarthurs was living there as principal tenants by 1802.

Ann's children were born in Islay, where Francis was employed as an Excise officer and writer, probably collecting duties from the various distilleries. Hamilton Campbell was born in 1812, Anne ('Lal') circa 1815 and Jemima Crawford circa 1821. The 1841 census shows another child in the household, four-year old Christian Campbell born in 1836 outside Islay (Hamilton's second name was also Campbell).[72] Hamilton was no longer living at home in Islay in 1841, but at Lethen House in Auldearn with the Brodies. Two Souter sisters, probably Francis' nieces, had recently married the two Brodie brothers in a romantic double ceremony. In 1845, Hamilton married the well-loved parish minister, William Barclay, a 54-year-old widower with young children. 'He was a fervid evangelical preacher, a keen theologian, devoted to pastoral duties,

---

[72] Julia Brackenbury also gave the middle name Campbell to one of her daughters.

and at the same time something of a doctor, lawyer and mechanic,'
George Bain wrote.

When Francis died, Ann and her daughter Ann moved from
Islay to the Auldearn manse. At one time they were joined there by
daughter Jemima, recently widowed, and her young family,
including Kate, who under her married name Sheppard would
become the southern hemisphere's greatest feminist.[73] The two
Mrs. Brodies had died by the time the litigation began, but their
husbands' and sons' prestige throughout Scotland would have given
Ann's claim credence.

---

[73] *Women's Suffrage: Kate Sheppard*, by P. Bunkle, Broadsheet Sept 1981. Kate Malcolm,
born in Liverpool in 1848, is described as gifted, beautiful and privileged. Her father,
Andrew Malcolm, died in 1862 in Jamaica. Her descendant, Tessa Malcolm, writes that
after his death, Kate lived in the household of her uncle, a minister, and became a lifelong
member of the Congregational Church. Jemima and her children emigrated to New
Zealand in 1868. Under her married name, Sheppard, Kate became a well-known feminist
in the first country in the world to obtain universal suffrage, and was depicted on a
national postage stamp and the $10 note.

CHAPTER SIX
LITIGATION FOR FAILLIE, GASK AND INVERERNIE

Miscarriage of justice?

Like the litigation for Dunmaglass, this case was also decided by the Court of Session at Edinburgh. In their condescendence, Souter and Noble claimed their ancestor Jean was the only daughter of William, the Captain Ban, and the only child who left lawful issue; they all denied that the Hon. John was grandson of Donald and Janet, sister of Farquhar of Dunmaglass. Lord Neaves closed the record in 1855, but it wasn't until the middle of 1858 that things were ready for what was called the 'debate between the parties' and judgment by jury.

But first, on 20 July, the judges debated an issue that in the future would be pondered by others, namely, as Ann's lawyers had asked: was there such a legal body as a clan?[74] Was Neil John right that only a member of Clan Chattan could own Faillie as the old feu-charter that the McBeans had from the Earl of Moray stipulated? With quick mocking humour and arcane language, the judges acknowledged they were unable to understand this Highland peculiarity. The issue was referred to an appropriate historian or man of law.

For the decision by jury concerning Faillie and the other properties, a number of witnesses had arrived in Edinburgh from Inverness. According to the *Inverness Advertiser*, Ann Souter and John Noble contested the claim that George Laidlaw Davidson M'Intosh descended from a sister of their ancestor, and denied that such a sister existed. If George Laidlaw could prove Lucy's

---

[74] M'Gillivray vs Souter p 19-20, *Tartans of the Clans* by Sir Thomas Innes of Learney: 'The clan as an institution has been thrice discussed in the Court of Session, in 1862 Lord Ardmillan in the Outer House delivered himself of a peroration upon clanship and feudalism, disfigured by really glaring errors in elementary legal history. The Inner House, Lord Colonsay presiding, confined themselves to holding that they did not find any such distinct statement of any practical qualification for membership of the clan as to exclude the heir-at-law'. Also discussed by Lords Currriehill and Deas.

existence, the inheritance would be split between all of them, because they were all descended from daughters of William, the Captain Ban. Although the *Inverness Advertiser* announced that the progress and result of the case would be of interest to their readers, they gave no further news of the two-day hearing. *The Scotsman*, on the other hand, published an article with a summary the day after the judgment was pronounced. The jury found for Ann Souter and John M'Gillivray Noble, and against George Laidlaw Davidson M'Intosh.

So the only claimant whose descent from the Captain Ban is today clear had lost. He had not abandoned the fight as had the grandchildren of Alexander in Ballintruan, and even now he did not give up. In May 1859 he was back in court claiming that the testimonies given by two of the witnesses in favour of Ann Souter and John Noble were no longer valid because William Smith, aged 87, and Archibald M'Gillivray, aged 77, both died before he became a party to the process. His objection was dismissed and there was nothing further he could do.

It is astonishing that George held out this long in court. The claimants had to provide proof of descent; there are no baptisms recorded in the parish registers for Lucy or her daughter, but neither are there for Jean or her children. What proof John or his son George provided is unknown. They had not denied that Jean was the daughter of the Captain Ban but rather that she was the only daughter who left issue. If they had denied Jean as a sister, they would probably have cut themselves off from all connection to the fortune given the sturdy proof in the form of copies of wills and letters showing that Jean was Lachlan's sister.

The two witnesses that George objected to, Archibald and William, were tenants of farms on the Dunmaglass estate. They were both of similar age to John Lachlan. If they held there was no Lucy, she may have died before they were born. But how could they not have known of Lucy's daughter, Janet Davidson, wife of the Moray forester at Darnaway Castle? It is unimaginable that the couple would not have presented their respects to this wealthy uncle at Dunmaglass, and that Lachlan, also keenly pursuing reforestation, would not have welcomed them openly. It seems passing strange that the Dunmaglass M'Gillivrays were so ignorant of their chief's kin. However, rather than ignorance, it may be deference to privacy that was at the origin of the widespread taciturnity that those brought up in the area, and still alive today, noted in their parents as regards genealogy and family relationships.

From Simon Mackintosh of Farr until today, clan genealogies and papers held by the Lyon Office in Edinburgh sanction Jean as sister of Lachlan and daughter of the Captain Ban. The 18th century documents that were found recently in the archives of Inverness showing that that William had a daughter Louisa but no Jean had not yet been unearthed; they may not have survived if they had. George Laidlaw Davidson M'Intosh had much expense in the defence of the authentic descent he claimed, but the money was ill-spent. This truly appears to be a miscarriage of justice.

While deploring the dismaying thought of a miscarriage of justice, we must allow for the possibility that the inheritance went to the rightful heirs after all. John Lachlan's fortune was inherited from Lachlan and Colonel John; it is reasonable their heirs should inherit if John Lachlan died without issue. Captain Ban's male descendants would have legal right to Dunmaglass, but not the properties purchased by Lachlan if he was not their kin. Any misunderstanding about inheritance would be due to faulty genealogies, and to the fact that Lachlan had undisclosed reasons for putting his properties in Dunmaglass' name. If Jean really was the sister of Lachlan – whatever their parentage – her heirs should inherit.

We do not know what paternity Lachlan himself claimed. The only relationship he clearly stated, in his memorial on oath drawn up in London in May 1784, in which he also declared that he was aged 65 and therefore born circa 1719, was that Colonel John was his nephew - an impossible relationship according to the traditional genealogies. In his own memorials, Captain William called Lachlan a near relation and then a cousin german. Lachlan took possession of the estate of Dunmaglass on his return from America, just as John took possession of Gask. We do not know whether they were entitled to do so, but both were willing to sink funds into a vast improvement programme for these two M'Gillivray properties.

What had the author of the genealogies to gain if the relationships he described were not genuine? Simon Fraser Mackintosh biased the genealogies against the descendants of

Donald the Tutor by simply disconnecting the latter from the Dunmaglass tree. Had he gone further and pushed a member of his mother's Dalcrombie branch into a closer position to the Dunmaglass family? Did he include Lucy in the family tree before or after the litigation? If it was pre-litigation, why was she not recognized by the jury – on his expert authority - as a legitimate daughter of the Captain Ban?

Those who stood to lose their claim to Dunmaglass on account of this misrepresentation of pedigree were the descendants of the five sons and two daughters of the Captain Ban. But, apart from Lucy, were there any? Did all the sons die on the battlefield of Culloden, or move to America or elsewhere? If there were descendants, had they sold their rights or were they cheated of their inheritance? Was the first to declare, Alexander in Urquhart, who would later drop his claim, a true descendant? The descendants of the pre-Culloden Dunmaglass family may have lived in reduced circumstances and no longer had claymores to wield. Here we remember the lawyers' opinion that Dunmaglass had not gone to the rightful heir and that somewhere there was a problem that bothered them.

Whatever the case, on 14 September 1858, Ann Macarthur Souter of Auldearn and John M'Gillivray Noble of Rahere Street, Goswell Road, London, upholsterer, obtained sasine as heirs portioners to John Lachlan M'Gillivray of Dunmaglass, 'their second cousin' (in fact second-cousin once-removed), of the town and lands of the wester plough of Gask and teinds, parish of Dunlichity, and half of the lands of Inverernie extending to 2 ploughs of land, within Strathnairn, on charter of confirmation by the curator to Francis, Earl of Moray, Sept 16, 1858.

A decision on Faillie was held up until a report was made on the nature of clans.

Coup de théâtre

Everything seemed settled, but it wasn't. Before any decision was made, a coup de théâtre brought drama and suspense to the proceedings. Scarcely a month after Souter and Noble were adjudged heirs to John Lachlan, an unexpected figure arrived from afar. This Jill-in-the-box claimant, making a late entrance on the stage, announced that she alone was lawful heir to John Lachlan's property.

Magdalene Julia Cutliffe Congreve Brackenbury was elder daughter of William M'Gillivray, director of the North West Company of Canada, whose Roy M'Gillivray ancestry we have previously seen. Julia and her sister Anne Maria were born in the first decade of the century and were brought up in the lap of Canadian luxury. Their aunt Mary came from Scotland to look after them when their mother died. They grew up gay and fun-loving, played the piano and egged on their father's guests to sing the risqué boat-songs of Canadian fur-trappers. William later bought them Pennyghael in Mull, the ancient homelands of the M'Gillivrays before part of the clan moved to Strathnairn; it was one of the few assets that escaped receivership when his Canadian empire collapsed. When William died in 1825, the two sisters moved from London to Hastings or Dover where they 'had cousins of whom they were very fond'.[75] Anne Maria married a fellow Canadian, and Julia shared their Kensington home in London until her romantic marriage in 1842 to the British vice-consul at Cadiz, William Congreve Cutliffe Brackenbury. The ceremony was held off the Spanish coast on board the HMS Malabar, fully decked for the occasion with officers and crew in resplendent uniforms. They had two sons in the 1840s (one would become admiral and commander of the Shah's Naval Brigade) and three daughters celebrated for their beauty and charm, Maule Campbell, Magdalena and Wilhelmina.[76]

---

[75] *McGillivray, Lord of the Northwest* by Marjory Wilkins Campbell. These cousins have not been identified. Coincidentally or not, Rev. Lachlan's sister married in Dover in 1847.

[76] *Burke's Landed Gentry*, 18th ed, vol 2 Magdalen lived in Spain and had the title 'Dona Excellentissima' conferred on her by Queen Cristina in recognition of the military services rendered by her husband, Sr. Manuel Delgado y Zuleta

This exotic Scottish claimant, born in Canada, living in Spain and married to an Englishman, arrived in October 1858. Although she was uncertain how her ancestor Benjamin tied into the Dunmaglass line, one week before Souter and Noble were due to be served heirs, her lawyers acted. On 6 June 1859 they informed Souter and Noble that they intended to have the earlier court judgment overthrown; the following day they presented a petition to the Sheriff court of Chancery claiming that Julia alone was nearest and lawful heir in special and in general to John Lachlan for the lands of Faillie, Gask and Inverernie.

That Julia was uncertain of how she tied in to the Dunmaglass family even after interrupting the procedure to declare her claim is clear from a letter that she wrote on 16 June 1859 to the laird of M'Intosh as 'head of the clan' to ask for his help in establishing her pedigree. She wrote that she had been in England the previous year on account of the death of the daughter of her late sister, and that certain friends had called her attention to the litigation. She added that her ancestor Benjamin was probably son of Farquhar McAllister, which of course makes nonsense of her argument that she was in a better position than the other litigants who were connected to the Dunmaglass family two generations later.

Explaining that she wanted to leave her young sons some land in 'Bonnie Scotland', she referred to M'Gillivray documents in his possession, remembering a visit to Moy with her father when she was a child, and talk of a chest containing interesting documents relating to the M'Gillivrays, whose key had been mislaid.

'It was not likely that (my grandfather) having lived in Scotland all his life could be under any mistake as to who was his grandfather…All my uncles and aunts have died away and certain claimants put aside this Benjamine some as dying unmarried, others as never existing, others as 4th son, others as illegitimate. (..) I would beg of you as Chief of the Clan if you could give any information as to the sons of Farquhar who existed in 1626. I have it stated that he had other sons, but I have been led to suppose that Benjamin my ancestor was the 2nd son and that Alexander the eldest son died unmarried abroad.'

These writings give one pause. Even though Julia was certain that her grandfather could not have made a mistake as to who his grandfather was, she may have been wrong. Ancestors' names are more familiar to women than to men, and in addition there may have been cause for confusion.

But as things now stood, considering Benjamin as quite remote, Julia could only believe that she was closest kin to the deceased chief to the exclusion of the other claimants by either contesting the genealogy that Ann Souter claimed, or by moving John Lachlan out of the Dunmaglass line into her Balnagaig family. If she was not able to do one of these two things, then she had more money than sense, but she would not have been her father's daughter.

Ann Souter had based her claim on Jean being daughter of the Captain Ban and perhaps to Julia's surprise, had won: Jean had successfully displaced Emilia and Lucy, the true daughters. Although Julia's tie-in to the Dunmaglass family was very uncertain, she could count on a closer relationship than Ann's. Besides, her Bean, son of Farquhar McAllister, would have been an ineffective link: Donald the Tutor had already been acknowledged eldest son in the earlier case for Dunmaglass. When Julia eventually submitted her genealogy some months later, she had moved Benjamin down two generations and claimed he was of the generation of the Captain Ban, but the more recent tie-in seemed incidental. Julia and her lawyers disregarded the fact that there was no documentary evidence of a brother named Benjamin.

If Julia planned to move John Lachlan into the Balnagaig line, he had to be closer to her grandfather Donald Roy than he was to Ann Souter's Duncan Roy. We shall explore this possibility, even though we may discard it as improbable. The order of precedence rules that inheritance goes downwards to the next son, skipping any daughters, while if the subject is the youngest son, the inheritance goes the next brother up. Julia's claim that she was in a more favourable position than Duncan's descendants meant that if William and Duncan Roy at Balnagaig were brothers, John Lachlan's ancestor was born after Duncan and before William or was the youngest son. If Duncan Roy and Donald Roy were brothers, John Lachlan's ancestor was similarly born after Duncan and before Donald, or was Donald or the youngest son.

Supposition 1

This would indicate that Benjamin was not the Captain Ban, as the latter had no son named Duncan.

BENJAMIN

WILLIAM m MARY dd by 1750

? — JOHN LACHLAN b 1782

DONALD ROY b 1740

WILLIAM of NWC, Canada b circa 1764

JULIA

DUNCAN ROY m JEAN M'GILLIVRAY

? — JOHN LACHLAN b 1782

MARY b 1767 m DONALD NOBLE

MARJORY b after 1767

JOHN NOBLE

JANET b circa 1757 m JOHN MACARTHUR in 1784

ANN b 1786 m FRANCIS SOUTER

Other siblings

Supposition 2

This would indicate that William had married Mary well before the 1740 bond giving her liferent over Balnagaig, or that Duncan Roy was very much younger than his wife, a putative daughter of Captain Ban born latest 1734.

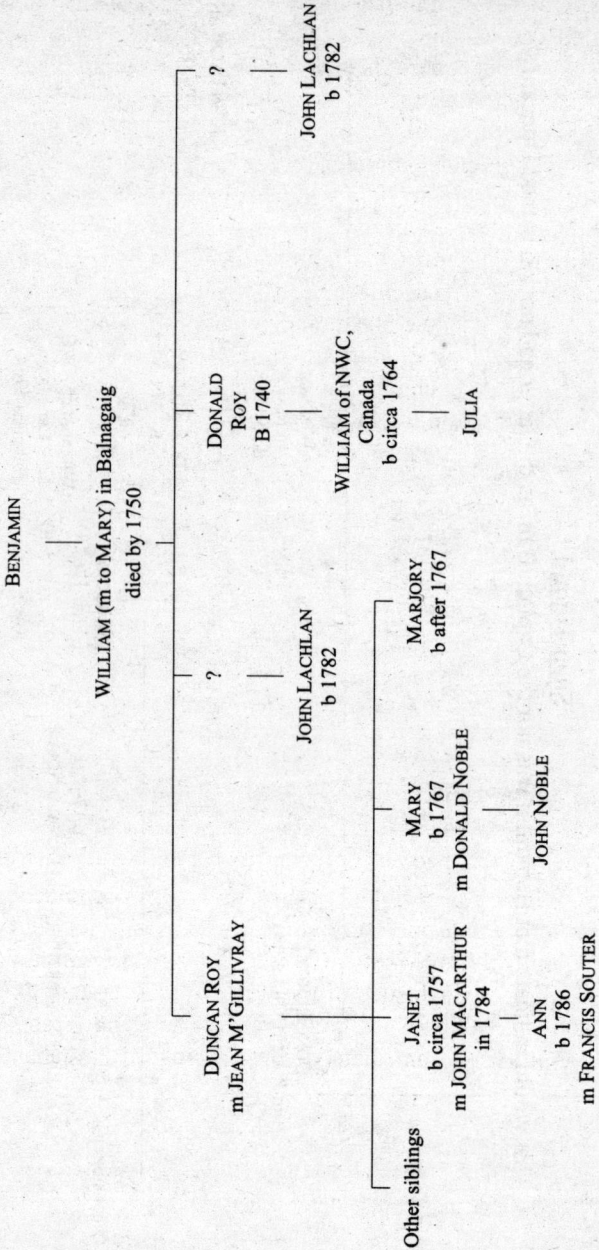

BENJAMIN

WILLIAM (m to MARY) in Balnagaig
died by 1750

DONALD ROY
B 1740

JOHN LACHLAN
b 1782

?

WILLIAM of NWC, Canada
b circa 1764

JULIA

?

JOHN LACHLAN
b 1782

MARJORY
b after 1767

MARY
b 1767
m DONALD NOBLE

JOHN NOBLE

DUNCAN ROY
m JEAN M'GILLIVRAY

JANET
b circa 1757
m JOHN MACARTHUR
in 1784

ANN
b 1786
m FRANCIS SOUTER

Other siblings

Based on the information at our disposal, this is the only reasoning that can explain Julia's claim of precedence if the hypothesis that she would contest Jean's pedigree seems improbable. It describes what the family structure may have been in Julia's opinion, and we presume she could back this. We would have to find other evidence indicating that John Lachlan was a member of the Balnagaig family to believe this to be a valid hypothesis. Here we should note that support for the fact there was a close blood relationship between the Roy M'Gillivrays and John Lachlan comes from an august quarter, an expert in genealogy, Sir Thomas Innes of Learney (1893-1971), Lord Lyon of Scotland. In an incidental comment in an article in *Scottish Notes & Queries*, he referred to William of Montreal as nephew to the chief.[77] Sir Thomas' father, Cosmo Innes, was closely involved in the litigation: it was he who had been commissioned to report on the nature of clans. The background to the case would have held no secrets for him. It is improbable that his son was misinformed, yet one wonders who he considered chief. It was unlikely to have been the young John Lachlan; so we must suppose it was his father William.

Changing the genealogy

No sooner had Julia set down her pedigree and the record was closed, than her lawyers legally queried whether she was to be tied to this record. They wanted to be able to change the genealogy described, not stick to what had been written down. This course, they argued, had been previously allowed in Scottish law courts.

Julia's genealogy is stated in her condescendence: she was the daughter and only surviving descendant of the late Hon. William M'Gillivray of Montreal, son of Donald M'Gillivray of Dalscoilt or Clovendale, a Justice of the Peace for the county of Inverness, and son of William M'Gillivray of Balnagaig, son of Benjamin M'Gillivray, immediate younger brother of Farquhar M'Gillivray of

---

[77] Volume IX, 3rd series, March 1931, The Innes Tartan, footnote 8. 'The arms of M'Gillivray recorded by a nephew of the chief in 1800 (...) Azure a galley, sails furled, oars in action (...) seem based on the arms of Cluny-Macpherson, whom they followed, but the presence of the galley will be noted as in the Macinnes arms.' Sir Thomas Innes of Learney.

Dunmaglass, grandfather of the said John Lachlan, last of Dunmaglass. Other records are oddly confusing. The minutes have Benjamin as grandfather of John Lachlan, an original way of reading Julia's statement. The judges made what appear to be erroneous genealogical statements, on one occasion referring to Julia as the first cousin thrice removed to John Lachlan.[78] In any event, Julia's statement concerning her genealogy matched what her father, William, declared in his Lyon Office statement. But, as we have stressed, there is no record of Farquhar and Emilia Steuart having a son Benjamin while there are numerous mentions of the Captain Ban, so her claim stood on very unsound ground.

Perhaps Julia now realised the similarity of the names Benjamin, Bean and the Captain Ban and accepted that her grandfather may have confused them, especially if William's first name was dropped. Julia's grandfather Donald Roy was born in 1740, some years after the latter's grandfather, if such he was, had died.

If Benjamin, Julia's ancestor, and the Captain Ban were one and the same person, the Balnagaig or 'Roy' M'Gillivrays were clearly closest kin to Dunmaglass. We know that the Captain Ban's children, Lachlan, Alexander, Charles, William, Farquhar, Louisa and Emilia, were born between 1714 and 1735, and that a William was main tenant at Balnagaig as early as 1746. Being Dunmaglass's first cousin may have made him eligible for the tenancy of the large farm at a relatively young age, or he may naturally have taken over

---

[78] a) Abstract states Mrs. Brackenbury is the daughter and only surviving descendant of Wm M'Gillivray of Montreal who is the son of Donald M'Gillivray of Clovendale Inverness-shire, son of Benjamin M'Gillivray of Dunmaglasss, the grandfather of John Lachlan of Dunmaglass. This shows that John Lachlan and William of Canada are cousins, as the Lord Lyon stated. b) First cousin thrice removed 21 December 1860 - Court of Session book Case No 37, pp 212 and 213: Julia was daughter William, son of Donald M'Gillivray (died about 1803), who was son of William M'Gillivray, tacksman of the farm of Balnagaick, and part of the estate of Dunmaglass, who died about (blank), and the said William M'Gillivray was the son of Benjamin M'Gillivray, immediate younger brother of the said Farquhar M'Gillivray of Dunmaglass, grandfather of the said late John Lachlan M'Gillivray. The judges, out of their depths in relationships, stated: 'The pursuer is thus first cousin thrice removed of the said John Lachlan M'Gillivray, the said Captain M'Gillivray, father of the said John Lachlan M'Gillivray, and the said William M'Gillivray of Balnagaig, the pursuer's great-grandfather, having been cousins-german, and the pursuer being third in descent from Wm of Balnagaig.'

from his father, a previous tenant, when he died in 1734. This seems a relatively plausible scenario as background to Julia's certainty of closest propinquity. Rather than shed light on the propinquity of the mysterious Jean, it makes her even more problematic. If Donald at Balnagaig was the infant John Lachlan's closest relative, and also Lachlan's nephew, why was he not appointed legal guardian? Why did this duty devolve to a supposedly elderly great-aunt with a dastardly husband of whom Lachlan greatly disapproved?[79]

None of these questions have answers, and it is difficult to favour one hypothesis over another. What is certain is that 150 years ago, the Dunmaglass tenants and lawyers knew more than we do today.

At the same time as presenting Julia's petition and advising of her intention to quash the earlier court decision in favour of Souter and Noble, her lawyers opposed the lifting of the judicial factory as the two successful claimants requested. Although the latter now had title to the lands of Easter Gask and half of Invererny, they were not yet able to claim the rental income.

The judges considered the petition from this late party 'who had not taken out in the competition, but who had been aware of the death of the common ancestor and who now claimed a preferable title to all the claimants.' They read Julia's statement: she and her husband had been resident abroad in Spain for many years. They had returned to Britain the previous October and immediately instituted the necessary enquiries to make formal proceedings for establishing Julia's rights as nearest and lawful heir of John Lachlan. She and her husband 'being strangers in Scotland, it was some time before they were enabled to collect the necessary materials, and put their case in shape'. This they had completed by June and had now returned to Spain, as Mr. Brackenbury could no longer be absent from his official duties. The Edinburgh judges were not amused and considered these late claimants tedious time-wasters.

The Lord President said:

---

[79] See letter from Lachlan to Jean in appendix

'It appears to me that this factory has subsisted long enough. The competition is now disposed of by a verdict in favour of one of the claimants. (…) there comes forward this claimant from Spain - not denying her knowledge of the death of the party who was last possessed of these lands, but, on the contrary, admitting her knowledge, and stating no reason for not having taken steps in vindicating her alleged right, except that she and her husband were living in a foreign country, and waited till they should have an opportunity of coming here and making personal inquiry into the matter, which they say was a more convenient way of making their inquiries than by employing an agent. If we were to recognise that as a ground for keeping up a factory of this kind, we may accept any excuse. It is said that the respondents could themselves make their legislation more cheaply than by employing an agent in the usual way. (..) Suppose we (delay) this factory for another six years, till this new claim is disposed of, another claimant might then appear, and after another course of six years' litigation a new claimant might again come forward from Spain, and still another from America, where parties generally come from to litigate for estates in this country. (..)'

The Court did not admit Julia's objection to Souter and Noble receiving the rentals from the estates. Her only hope now was that the law courts would overturn the previous judgment.

Closed record

When all had seemed settled, Ann Souter and John Noble's lawyers were back in the fray. They did not treat Julia's claim as extravagant and far-fetched, but handled the matter of new or different genealogies with extreme caution. They objected going to litigation to argue the unrestricted issue of whether Julia was the nearest and lawful heir in special and in general to John Lachlan. The terms were too general. 'It would be dangerous and unjust to the defenders to send the case to trial upon these general issues proposed by Mrs. Brackenbury. In this case there was the more necessity for putting the propinquity in the issue that there was reason to apprehend that the pursuers might attempt to prove a different case from that set forth on record.'

They wanted something 'tangible' to argue, for example: a) that Julia was the great-great-grandchild of Benjamin, younger brother of Farquhar and b) whether, this being the case, she was nearest and lawful heir.

John Noble and Ann Macarthur Souter (cousins) and Julia Brackenbury, whose lawyers argued in the Edinburgh's solemn courts, were second cousins through their Roy great-grandfather. On the Dunmaglass side, Souter and Noble had a strong recognizable ancestor, whereas wherever Benjamin was placed, Julia did not. Yet Souter and Noble were anxious that she should not be able to change the record as it would be dangerous and unjust.

Julia's lawyers replied that they were perfectly willing to be controlled and limited by the record; but it was 'unreasonable, and not at all necessary in order to confine them to the case that Julia should be compelled to put in issue, word for word, her whole allegation of propinquity. It was by virtue of her descent that she was nearest heir of John Lachlan – to the exclusion of all others.'

On 21 December 1860 the judges in the 1st Division under Lord Ardmillan met solely to debate a strange request: was Julia bound to keep to the closed record, to the genealogy she had described? As it was officially put: Is a general issue controlled by the record? Below are extracts from Lord Ardmillan's lengthy peroration:

'The point which we have to determine is: What is the matter that is the true question here in issue between the parties, and what it is that we are to send to trial? (…) It was stated to us that the reason why the general mode of putting the issue was objected to was, that under it the party might endeavour to establish, and might perhaps be permitted, or entitled to establish, a pedigree not identical with that set forth.

If, under all circumstances, it were disclosed – if it should appear that that other pedigree excluded all other persons and made her nearest heir, the pursuer did not say that it might not be part of her object, in the course of the trial, to take advantage of that state of matters. On the contrary, I understand the argument to be that the pursuer did not wish to be excluded from that event, and from trying that question. We are here, therefore, dealing with a case where a general form of issue is asked, under an express avowal that the party so asking it has in contemplation to try a different pedigree from that which she has set forth on record.

(…) But this much is very clear, that a party coming into court with a particular pedigree – on which the record is closed – and seeking, not only to reduce another party's title, but with her own claim to be heir in special – would not be entitled to go into another pedigree in order to establish her right in some other way, else what is the use of a record? That I think is perfectly clear. Therefore, if we wish to determine the true question at the trial, we must put the issue in such a way as would exclude that attempt. (…) I think it would not be safe to send the case to trial on that general issue proposed by the pursuer.

Another reason is this: that in this case, with the parties that are here, and the number of statements, the pedigree is a good deal confused, and the jury might have difficulty in following it, and it is therefore desirable that they should have before them, in a brief form, the precise point which they are going to try. Now the pedigree which Mrs. Brackenbury sets forth is in accordance with that stated by the pursuer in article 4 of the condescendence. I think it right that the pursuer's pedigree should, in a short form, be stated in the issue, and I also think that the one proposed by the defender does so state it, and therefore that the issue proposed by the defender is the proper issue for trying this case.'

Lord Ardmillan's formal judgment was that the propinquity of a pursuer, as stated on record, ought - so long as there exists doubt whether issues are controllable by reference to the record - to be set forth in the issues, and especially where there is ground for apprehending that the pursuer may attempt to prove at the trial a different pedigree from that set forth on record.

That is all that has survived on the case. We do not know what happened afterwards, whether Julia continued with her case and was unsuccessful. Perhaps she dropped her claim after Lord Ardmillan's pronouncement, or perhaps the case was described in a remit that was recalled. Whatever course of action Julia chose, she did not win.

It has been posited that Julia's desire to introduce new genealogies stemmed from doubts about the place of Benjamin in the M'Gillivray genealogies. But she could not move Benjamin either forwards or backwards to her advantage, and her dependence on Benjamin seems incidental as we have seen. It is difficult to believe that she would engage in costly litigation with no proof or knowledge of the matter. She had known about John Lachlan's death and yet only participated in the litigation when Jean was recognized as daughter of the Captain Ban. It is clear she had different genealogies to put forward than what she had put down on record, and these were dangerous for the other claimants. Somehow she did things badly or was fainthearted. And Ann Souter, with her impressive connections, as we have seen, was surely the most respectable of the motley collection of claimants in anybody's eyes.

Clan as legal entity

If Julia's court case was not reported in the press, the subsequent one received much attention. This was for the lands of Faillie and the possible restriction that they were destined to members of Clan Chattan. It has been widely commented on by different historians and lawyers, for the pronouncement raised the hackles of a number of observers. In the neo-romantic upsurge of everything Scottish and Queen Victoria's affection for the country, national dignity returned. The particularity of clans was one reason for pride. Would 'Clan Chattan lands' have any meaning in law?

Two years earlier, Lord Ardmillan had summarily admitted that, in the 17th century, Lord Moray may have had an object in inserting this clan clause, but 'this membership of the clan is a very evanescent matter, it is difficult to seize hold of it...' So they had assigned Cosmo Innes, Esq[80], to investigate and report on 'What a clan was, are there now any clans, is there such a thing as Clan Chattan, is membership transmitted exclusively through males?' Cosmo Innes was a leading legal historian and sheriff depute for Moray and Nairn, another close close acquaintance of the Brodies of Lethen and godfather to Hamilton's cousin's son, James Campbell Brodie, born in 1848.

We do not know what Cosmo Innes reported, because his remit was recalled 'to the regret of historians', as his son Sir Thomas Innes of Learney wrote in *Tartans of the clans and families of Scotland*. But Neil John lost. The legal existence of clans was not recognised in law. Ten years after their distant cousin's death and after protracted litigation, Souter and Noble, according to the register of sasines, were given the town and lands of Faillie and others as 'heirs portioners of John Lachlan M'Gillivray, last of Dummaglass their (blank)'. The relationship was too complicated for the scribe to work out.

---

[80] Cosmo Innes had at one time worked as a lawyer together with Charles Fraser Mackintosh, one of his relations.

CHAPTER SEVEN
DÉNOUEMENT

The aftermath

There was further litigation between Neil John and Ann Souter concerning the boundaries between their properties, with Thomas Brodie representing Ann. But eventually she and her cousin John Noble sold their windfall lands and banked the money. The 1851 census ten years earlier showed John Noble with his wife Mary Ann and his children aged between one and sixteen, Maria (seamstress), Alexander, Eliza, John, Ellen and Emily, living at Clerkenwell Close in London. In the 1861 census, John Noble no longer appears in the bustle of the Victorian Rahere street and the neighbourhood of artisans, compass-makers, goldchain polishers, watchmakers and racket-stringers and women folding books, envelopes and feathers.

Whether he continued to work as an upholsterer is not known; he died in 1869, and half the proceeds of the sale of the property went into a trust for his heirs, and legacies for his three sisters and their children.

Though they were neighbours, the second cousins were worlds apart socially. Ann Macarthur Souter, her widowed daughter Hamilton and her grandchildren moved from the manse in Auldearn to Hay Lodge in Nairn. The 1861 census shows Hamilton, fund holder, living with her children Mary Catherine, Annie, Hamilton, Williamina and William, and mother Ann Souter, widow, age 74, also fund holder. William Barclay had died and the children of his first marriage were elsewhere. His will in 1857 indicated that his family was expecting inheritance of the Dunmaglass property, and that William trusted his debts would be paid off by this.

At the windblown cemetery next to Auldearn church, set on a flat-topped mound above the rooftops of the village houses, there is a private enclosure for the Dunbar and Brodie families. Here too are buried Rev. William Barclay, his wife, children and mother-in-law. Ann's tombstone carries the name 'Ann Souter'. There is no maiden name, which is unusual in Scotland where gravestones carry both maiden and married names.

Although the *Nairnshire Telegraph* in 1857 reported the Neil John and Rev. Lachlan case, it did not mention the second court case. If the Nairn historian George Bain was aware of litigation, he did not refer to it, only mentioning that William Barclay's wife, Hamilton, was connected to the Brodies of Lethen. Perhaps the litigation was considered distasteful in this small Victorian town, fast becoming a fashionable resort. It was not unusual to hush up what a prim society might deem uncomely: the divorce proceedings of the daughter of their relation, Sir James Mackintosh, who had run off with her lover, were held in closed chambers and nothing was published in deference to her celebrated father. Besides, in this instance, who were the M'Gillivrays? Lord Macaulay, whose grand-uncle had been minister in Cawdor, described them through English eyes. They 'could not talk a Christian tongue' and 'had only lately begun to wear Christian breeches'. Worse, the fortune being claimed was built on the sale of trinkets, rifles and alcohol to Indians and the trade of African slaves in chains. This was not a background that the wife of a minister, a relation of the Brodies, would refer to with pleasure or pride.

A neighbour of Ann Souter's daughter Jemima in New Zealand was Rev. Lachlan, who had wrung the inexplicable financial compromise out of Neil John. He had traveled apparently first to Canada, then back to Nairn in 1859, and finally to New Zealand the following year. Here he worked as a missionary for nine months before taking up farming. Predictably, because Neil John was much in debt, Lachlan was not fully paid and in 1863 he sued for the balance owing. Meanwhile, his lawyer was pressing for payment. Lachlan reminded him that he had agreed to waive his fees if he was not successful. Thomson replied: 'You have got or will receive under the arrangement with the successful claimant a large sum of money, say £3000, and this sum you could not have got but for my successful research and the skilful use made of (it) at the trial.' So the lawyer took almost half Rev. Lachlan's booty.

Reverend Lachlan turned to politics and became the first mayor of Riverton, then, in 1873, was elected to the House of Representatives as Member for the Wallace constituency. In his old age he suffered from ill health, and, when he died, was buried at the Kaiapoi cemetery where his gravestone reads: 'In Memory of Lachlan M'Gillivray. Late MHR for Riverton. Last of the Daviot Family. Died 1st August 1880, aged 71 years. By grace ye are saved.'

George Laidlaw Davidson M'Intosh returned to his young wife and books in Kirkcaldy, undoubtedly a poorer man. He continued as an auctioneer until he moved to St Andrews in 1862 where he opened a bookshop and published the *St Andrew's Gazette and Fifeshire News* for its proprietors for a year (1863-64). He died there in 1878. The bookshop continued under his widow Jane Johnstone.

Although according to the parish records George had a son William in 1853, he does not seem to have been survived by any children. In his holograph will, he leaves whatever effects may remain after his wife's death to his nephew's son, William Adamson, and a young relative of his wife's. His nephew, John Adamson, born in 1828, lived in Selkirk then Glasgow where he was keeper of St. Mark's Hall, and, possibly in a dismayed attempt to keep his real genealogy alive when the courts had thrown it out, he loaded a string of ancestral names on his infant offspring: a daughter born in 1863 was christened Frances Lucy M'Gillivray Davidson Adamson. She should have been the proud Dunmaglass heiress; instead, in the 1881 census, she appears as a modest shop girl in Glasgow.

Neil John's legacy

The first thing Neil John did on succeeding to Dunmaglass was build an elegant manor he named Dunmaglass Lodge. It was close to where Balnagaig had stood, in secluded hills above the fast-flowing stream, a mile or two from the old farmhouse of Dunmaglass. Despite the tenants' enthusiasm about their new landlord, and his profession of holding their interests close to his heart, he did not remain in Strathnairn but returned to Glengarry. Only in 1880 did the family return to Scotland for Neil John's last years as an invalid.[81] He died in 1886, aged only 58. An Episcopal

---

[81] *MacGillivray Clan book*. Neil John and his wife are not in the 1881 census.

service was held at Dunmaglass, after which a hearse drawn by four black horses took his body to Dunlichity, nine miles distant. After a second church service, he was buried in the grave of his grandfather, Farquhar of Dalcrombie. The obituary that appeared in the Inverness papers was eulogistic: he had been genial and kindly, won the respect of all who had the pleasure of his acquaintance and took a quiet but intelligent interest in imperial and country affairs. He was a thoughtful neighbour, excellent landlord, and possessed a generous heart. 'His popularity as landlord and neighbour was strikingly shown on the occasion of his son's coming of age, an event which is in recent remembrance.'

When Neil John's accounts were examined, it was discovered that he had nothing but debts, and Dunmaglass, the ancient home of the M'Gillivrays, was owned by creditors. The family was penniless.

The sons failed to make a success of indigo or tea plantations in the East Indies. Younger son, Angus, died destitute in Australia at the beginning of the century. Colonel Sopper, the new proprietor of Dunmaglass Lodge who for some reason had 'wantonly destroyed' the original old farmhouse, apparently sent money to Australia to meet the funeral expenses. Angus' twin sister, Mary Augusta, married in Canada. In 1914, the older son John William, living in lodgings in London, was also destitute and suffering from acute consumption. He died on 18 September that year in the ignominy of a London workhouse or drowned in the Thames.

Eight years after his death, a certain Gerald Edmondson, a Sherlock Holmes-type with an excellent memory, eager to make money where he could, wrote three extremely odd but dramatic letters from St Philip Vicarage, 1 Queens Square, London SW8.[82] These letters are now held in the Lyon Office in Edinburgh. Who he was writing to and the whereabouts of 'the book' he refers to are a mystery. Three pages, presumably extracts from this book, are stapled to these letters: they are the account of the court proceedings that we have included above. The letters describe the final years of the last Dunmaglass. He appears as a ghostly, doomed figure who had lost everything save the genealogies of the M'Gillivray clan,

---

[82] This address does not seem to be a vicarage in the postal directory of the period.

which were the last and most precious of his possessions. Despite this, he made no arrangements for their safekeeping after his death. Instead he simply abandoned them in his landlady's house and if they really did exist, would presumably now be in some dusty archive of the Lyon Office.

Dec. 6th, 1922

Dear Sir,

In 1914 a Mr. M'Gillivray quitted apartments rented to him by my mother without making payment and left behind a book on the 'Proceedings in the competing petitions as heir-male to John Lachlan M'Gillivray between Neil John M'Gillivray and the Reverend Lachlan M'Gillivray before Lord Neaves in 1857'.

The book is in good condition, no leaves are missing and the genealogical tree is intact.

If the matter is of interest to you, I shall be pleased to give further details.

Yours faithfully,

Gerald Edmondson (typed)

***

Jan. 8th, 1923

Dear Sir,

Mr. John M'Gillivray owed to my mother £5.17.6d of which you may pay such part as you think fit.

You will forgive me for laying upon you the onus of fixing a price, but my present insecure position as a temporary Civil Servant would certainly prejudice my judgment.

Yours faithfully,

Gerald Edmondson (typed)

***

Jan. 16th, 1923

Dear Sir,

Perhaps I put things rather crudely in my last letter. I think if I give you more details, you will not consider your clansman's defection so very unworthy.

Mr. John M'Gillivray rented a room from my mother during the winter of 1914. He was a tall lean man of evident culture. Other than a small paper covered parcel, he possessed no luggage.

Each morning, after a cup of tea and a piece of dry toast, he had a cold tub. Nothing more substantial than tea and toast passed his lips so far as we could tell. I saw him once in a teashop about midday and before him was tea and toast.

For some weeks he appeared to be rapidly losing flesh. His eyes became brilliant and the region of his cheek bone assumed a feverish flush. He coughed more frequently at night and from the dampness of his sheets and the browny red streak in his sputum. I surmised advanced T.B.

His mode of life, however, continued: tea and toast followed by a cold tub. One day he failed to return and a blotting pad in his room showed these few words

…have tried…either the river now or the workhouse…

My mother twice offered him something more substantial than the eternal tea and toast but he firmly refused.

Believe me, my mother so far from feeling injured by his abrupt departure, was truly sorry he had not accepted her well-meant offers; as for his bill, all thoughts of it were dismissed entirely from her mind. He certainly had grit. I'm certain he had not even a shilling on the day he left but his bearing was as purposeful as Lucifer's must be. I'd like to think that I could touch bottom and retain as much pride.

I am afraid my mother would be disappointed in me could she but know how I approached you. Anyway, your cheque helped me out of a tight corner for which I'll say nothing more flowery than Thank You.

Yours gratefully,

Gerald Edmondson

The housekeeper heiress

Charlotte, the housekeeper with the windfall inheritance from John Lachlan, bought a house in Inverness, but she did not live long. The Clarks were a pious and church-going family; a sister appears at the family home in Margaret Street in 1881 as manageress of the National Bible Depot. When Charlotte died in 1859, at about the time that Julia made her appearance, her remains were interred as John Lachlan had instructed, next to her former employers, and a new inscription was added to the marble: 'Also in memory of Charlotte Clark, their faithful and attendant servant during 29 years. Died 05.07.1859'

Charlotte instructed her executors to keep £2,000 in trust for two good schools in the parish of Daviot and Dunlichity, where those of the name M'Gillivray would have free instruction. A school was built a school at Nairnside on land that M'Intosh of Raigmore donated. It was a surprising location, within the boundary of the parish only a mile from the battlefield of Culloden, but quite inaccessible to children from Dunmaglass. The School Board of Daviot & Dunlichity took it over in 1872 and criticized the trustees for siting the school where it benefited few families in the parish and many more in adjoining Inverness and Croy. They were also surprised when they could not easily obtain information about the trust funds used to set it up. Some years later it was turned over to the Inverness authorities and existed till 1948 when it closed with only seven pupils, while the school at Dunmaglass closed in 1947 with only three pupils.

Speculation

In the distant and remote countryside of Strathnairn in the 18th century, a tenant farmer may last have seen Dunmaglass in the late 1750s when he left with his regiment for the East Indies. The effective head of the family was Farquhar M'Gillivray of Dalcrombie; he collected the rents, and if asked, could give news of the absent landlord. Then in 1783, a wealthy gentleman in his 60s, silk-stockinged and and perhaps bewigged like the Inverness notables, appeared and settled in the old house where Dunmaglass' sister Anne also lived. With him were one or two children aged one or two; the boy, whose birth was not recorded in a parish register, was presented as the M'Gillivray scion. The old gentleman was devoted to the lad, introduced as the orphaned son of his relative, the M'Gillivray chief who had not reappeared. The child, John Lachlan, was the infant proprietor of Dunmaglass. Most importantly, Anne and Dalcrombie concurred and called the gentleman Mr. Lachlan.

Was any child of equal value to a son of his own or William's? If so, perhaps it was quite different. The gentleman of Savannah may have appeared at Dunmaglass, collected a child from the farm of Balnagaig up the valley, not a sister's child, for any sister was well past child-bearing by then, but another relative's. Whoever the parents, the child was finely dressed, educated, introduced to Inverness society as Lachlan's protegé, the new M'Gillivray chief, 'my relation'.

Was Lachlan himself a scion of one of the Dalcrombie lines? In this case, he was most likely named after Lachlan, his M'Intosh grandfather of Daviot, was brother of Alexander and Archibald and may have brought back from America his niece Jean, who was born in 1737 in Dalzeil. Jean was Lachlan's daughter or niece, local M'Gillivrays whispered until a generation or two ago.[83] Although Alexander in Knocknagael's daughter Jean survived till adulthood

---

[83] William MacGillivray, Auldearn

and may have spent her childhood in America, we know nothing about her apart from greetings to 'Miss Jeanie' in letters from family friends.

There are many hypotheses, including the one that Emilia, daughter of the Captain Ban, changed her name to Jean, and that Lucy and her daughter were rejected by her brothers and sister.

Lachlan the Indian trader had wealth but, in principle, he couldn't buy Dunmaglass: it was entailed from father to son or assignee in the old 17th century deeds of the property from the Thanes of Cawdor. There was nothing that a more successful branch of M'Gillivrays could do to acquire the lands and chiefship of the clan except creep closer on the genealogical tree if there were branches to bypass. But then, was anything really any different, we may ask ourselves. From the beginning of clan history, power would sit in the lap of those who were determined to wield it. Legal niceties were but modern and incidental trivia.

John Lachlan's relatives in the Hebrides

The history of these Dunmaglass M'Gillivrays might well have ended there, after a tale of reversals of fortune, riches that had been made in the new world, trafficking in slaves, plantations and trading with Creeks, risks run, dangers faced and profits banked – all this so that a powerful M'Gillivray family might rise in Strathnairn. Instead, the fortune was used a hundred years later for the early emancipation of New Zealand women, the extravagances of a Canadian adventurer and the restless wanderings of a Scottish minister. If the desire to acquire wealth was based on aspirations for the betterment of the next generation, such dreams were in vain, bursting like insubstantial bubbles when the young forged their own destiny. If 'poor' John Lachlan was a victim of his ancestors' expectations for a new dynasty, he defied their example and aspirations: he had no lawful children, and never lived on the property they left.[84]

He had no brothers and no M'Gillivray first cousins; as the male lines of his grand-uncles born at the end of the 17th century had died out, he had only distant M'Gillivray relations through his great-aunt Janet, married to Donald of Dalcrombie, and perhaps the obfuscated descendants of William, the Captain Ban.

Although traditional genealogies and the litigation show that there were no close M'Gillivray relatives, astonishingly, they appear. The inventory of John Lachlan's papers at his death shows each tack, bank account, trusteeship or voucher he held. At least one packet of documents was not kept or not listed; it would have contradicted the traditional description of the family – John Lachlan

---

[84] There is a report from Canada and confirmed in Scotland that when a widower, John Lachlan fathered a son who grew to resemble him so that he was dispatched with his mother to a far corner of the globe, China or Canada.

had close relations in the most remote and distant corner of Scotland.

Between 1793 and 1797, a young William M'Gillivray studied medicine at Aberdeen University. Nothing is known about his origins, but when a student, he had a 'natural' son born on 25 January 1796 with a local lass, Ann Wishart. He named the child William. When the child was three, he was sent to the care of his father's brothers and sisters in a remote Hebridean community where wildlife abounded and where his interest in birds was born; he would become the celebrated ornithologist reputed for his classification of Scottish birds.

The family had no early connection with the island of Harris, and the older William's parents are traditionally but uncertainly held to be incoming farmers in the 1790s. It is surprising to find a well-heeled family of M'Gillivrays here given the sheer remoteness of the islands. Also surprisingly, Provost Phineas M'Intosh of Drummond and his nephew Angus M'Intosh of Holm bought lands here in 1808, their only investment outside the town of Inverness.

The young child from Aberdeen arrived circa 1800 and when he later wrote of his childhood, he never referred to grandparents. Perhaps it was William and his brothers who, despite their youth, held the valuable tack to Northtown, one of the most substantial farms on the southwest tip of Harris.[85]

Harris had passed out of the hands of the MacLeods of Dunvegan in 1779 and was now held by Captain Alexander MacLeod of Berneray, but the latter's papers were lost in a fire, so no written account of the tenancy has survived. At the turn of the century, when William was in the army, this wild, remote island was home to his three-year-old son from Aberdeen and his brothers and sisters: 25-year old John (born 1775-1780) - who was older than William - two young girls, Marion and Marcella or Marjory and

---

[85] With a rental of £170 in 1818. The first reference to this family is not until 1813, when Roderick is shown as tenant of Northton and the tack of the farm legally belonged to William's second son.

fifteen-year-old Roderick, who would declare that William was his next older brother german.[86]

Although Aberdeen University records show that William was a student in 1797, there are also various references to a William M'Gillivray in the army at this time. One enrolled in the 33rd Foot on Christmas Day in 1796 as assistant surgeon under the future Duke of Wellington. William of Harris is referred to after his death as sometime surgeon in the 31st Regiment of Foot, but we do not know when he started his military career.[87]

William soon married Euphemia ('Effie') MacNeill, daughter of William MacNeill of Pabbay and sister of Major Donald MacNeill.[88] Perhaps it was only now that the family bought the well-stocked farm of Northton. A son, Donald William, was born some time after 1805. He was still an infant and his half-brother at Aberdeen, where he had been sent two years previously aged eleven, when their father, whose regiment had been engaged in the Pensinsular wars, died on 11 October 1809. Though never mentioning his father or his grandparents in his journals that have survived, William would recollect his life with his uncle when he returned from university.

After William's death, Euphemia and her son lived at her parent's home in Pabbay. William's brother Roderick applied to become his nephew's tutor, and then in Euphemia's words 'thought proper to possess himself, without any legal authority, of a well-stocked farm held by his deceased brother and to manage and administer the same for his own behoof'.

Roderick was appointed tutor in October 1811 to his nephew Donald William, but was inattentive, it seems, to his ward's

---

[86] Ages are based on the 1841 census, with 5 years added. Roderick was over 25 in 1811 when he became tutor.

[87] Military records refer to various or the same William M'Gillivray at this time. In 1804 a William joined the Cameron Highlanders (79th Foot) and next year on half-pay with the 4th Foot. In 1808 a William was on full-pay with the 14th Dragoons. The following year a William was promoted Surgeon with the 60th Foot (King's Royal Rifle Corps). Farquhar of Dalcrombie's son, William (born in the mid 60s), was also in the army; according to Farr in the 71st, and died unmarried at the farm of Dell.

[88] According to Hebrides historian Bill Lawson, Effie was daughter of William MacNeill and Marjory MacLeod, probably a McLeod of St Kilda, and maybe a hitherto unrecorded half-sister of Alexander McLeod, last MacLeod tacksman of St. Kilda.

interests. He omitted to draw up inventories of the child's assets. His cautioner until 1816 was Mr. Campbell, a successful merchant at nearby Ensay, who lent considerable sums to the MacLeods of Harris and Dunvegan. He also had dealings with a business partner and close friend of William of the North West Company, Isaac Todd, who held two lots of several thousand acres close to George Town on Prince Edwards Island in Canada. When Todd sold these lands in 1808, he empowered Campbell at Ensay to act for him. This is either a coincidence, or by recommendation from William. In the latter event, it would be an indication of some close relationship between the Roy M'Gillivrays and the five young people on the remote island of Harris.

Euphemia watched this younger brother of her deceased husband and her stepson in possession of the farm where she had perhaps once lived, and accused them of 'dilapidating' the assets that legally belonged to her infant son. She described Roderick's failure to assess the value and extent of her child's property as 'very reprehensible conduct', pointing out that he 'allowed nearly six years to elapse before he took any steps in the business... At long last he thought of bestirring him in the matter though not till after much of the pupil's means had been applied by him to his own use.' Relations between Euphemia and her brother-in-law became acrimonious. She accused Roderick of having 'grossly abused the trust committed to him'; he was 'guilty of a most culpable dereliction of duty' and she judged him unfit for the office he had assumed. Roderick's replies were drafted by Campbell M'Intosh, one of John Lachlan's curators and a trusted friend and factor of the M'Gillivrays of Dunmaglass.

Euphemia took steps to have Roderick removed as tutor while he hastily tried to make up these inventories. The procedure for inventories was the same as it had been for the child John Lachlan, and involved the tutor summoning the next of kin on both the mother's and the father's sides.

On 16 June 1818, Roderick raised an Edict against John Lachlan M'Gillivray, Esquire of Dunmaglass and Donald M'Gillivray, drover at Aberchalder, persons nearest in kin to the pupil on the father's side, and William MacNeil of Pabbay and his son Major Donald MacNeil on the mother's side.

Dunmaglass and Donald M'Gillivray answered the summons. They did not deny they were next of kin. Instead, like Euphemia, they chastised him for the 'inexcusable delay' in making these inventories. Roderick replied that 'in the very remote part of the country where he lives, and the effects of the deceased were situated, this could not be avoided.'

John Lachlan and his relative Donald seemed to prevaricate by arguing that Roderick had not produced the necessary Factory. Roderick pointed out he could not make necessary decisions in his tutorial duties without immediate action from them, and they were prejudicing the child's education. Roderick then complained to William Fraser-Tytler, sheriff depute of Inverness:

'The objectors state that there is not sufficient evidence produced of the Pursuer's authority for acting, that the attestation of a Minister in the remote Island of Harris is not sufficient but that every kind of hazard in the transmission of valuable papers must be experienced to satisfy the objectors but it is hoped your Lordship will not be inclined to indulge in such captious objections to stop a tutor in the management of the afffairs of his ward.'

Euphemia, meanwhile, was successful in removing her brother-in-law as tutor by a process in the Court of Session and subsequently took over as Factrix loco tutoris in 1818. Even so, the sheriff-substitute forced John Lachlan and Donald 'under penalty of certification' to make up inventories, just as Roderick resigned his office, disclaiming all intention of interfering further in the minor's affairs.

Northton passed from William, surgeon, to his legitimate son, Donald William. It was sold by 1830 when Roderick and his brother John, and their nephew William lived on a smaller farm in Rusigary, the northern township of the island of Berneray. Hebrides historian Bill Lawson laments the lack of information about the family and writes: 'There are no records of burials here of any of the family, though there are some caibeals - small burial enclosures - around the Church at Rodel whose names are not now known, but then the M'Gillivrays were so disliked here that you would think that they would have been remembered.'

William the ornithologist

Despite Roderick's concerns about the education of his nephew, Donald William's schooling was sound. He joined his elder half-brother at Edinburgh University where he studied medicine. Later, he was both a doctor and farmer, first at Ormiclate, then at Eoligarry with its 3,000 acres of land. In 1851 Donald William, Esquire of Eoligarry married Christian, daughter of Murdoch McLellan, a South Uist farmer, and had two sons, Murdoch and William. The sons eventually emigrated to Australia. Roderick's sister Marion married Angus McKay, and at Gorbals, near Glasgow, had sons Murdoch and Angus.

William, ornithologist, married the younger sister of his uncle Roderick's wife and became a renowned professor of Natural History at Aberdeen.[89] From an early age, he showed great interest in science and birds and, in 1818, while his uncle Roderick was engaged in legal proceedings with Dunmaglass involving his younger brother, he undertook a marathon walk from Aberdeen to London to further his field knowledge of natural sciences. He slept under the open skies, and recorded his observations.

William was a hard man on others, but spared himself even less. 'My shoes and stockings were in tatters so that the gravel was getting in and tormenting me.' He completed the last lap of fifty-eight miles in one stretch on nothing but bread and an apple, sitting to rest his feet every two or three miles, the last twelve hours in torrential rain, soaked to the skin. He arrived in London almost on his knees and wrote: 'I have now finished my journey, and I am satisfied with my conduct.'

'He had not much the appearance and manners of the gentleman. I had much interesting natural-history talk with him, and he was very kind to me,' wrote Charles Darwin who made his acquaintance some years later.

---

[89] The couple had thirteen children: at least one emigrated to Australia and was a doctor of medicine, a second was a noted naturalist and joined several voyages of discovery to the South Pacific and east coast of Australia.

The link with Dunmaglass

It is startling to discover that John Lachlan and Donald were next-of-kin to these Harris M'Gillivrays, and baffling to work out how. Donald was a drover, cattle dealer and tenant of Balnacarnish of Aberchalder and lived above his means. When he went bankrupt in 1821, his assets of £150 were lodged in the hands of Archibald McTavish of Garthbeg, Donald Roy's son-in-law, to distribute among the creditors, suggesting a link with the Roy M'Gillivrays.

When Roderick in Harris summoned his ward's relatives, he had to follow a specific procedure. By the 1672 Tutors and Curators Act (which still subsists), the two next of kin by the father, and the two by the mother, are always cited; and when the tutor is himself one of the next of kin, he must cite the two who are next in degree to the minor after himself. A younger brother will take precedence, and where there is none, the next older brother. Were then Donald in Aberchalder and John Lachlan of Dunmaglass next older brothers of surgeon William who died in the Peninsular wars?

We will not think this is the case when we consider the ages of the Hebrides family. William would have been about 14 years old when he enrolled at Aberdeen University in 1793, although he may have been older or younger like his own son William who was already there aged twelve. William, surgeon, was most likely born between 1776 and 1781. Roderick, who was born circa 1786, declared in the Act of Tutorship in 1811 that William was his immediate senior surviving brother. If we do not think that John Lachlan, born 1782, was a brother, we must posit that John, the eldest brother in the Harris family – ten years older than Roderick - who was alive but not summoned, was incapax. Yet neither of William's sisters was summoned either.[90] Whatever their relationship to John Lachlan, what is certain is that it was close.

There is no place for surgeon William and his siblings related to Dunmaglass in the traditional genealogies. Neither did Donald William come forward to claim Dunmaglass in the 1850s litigation

---

[90] A consideration is that the next-of-kin summoned should perhaps be living within the jursidction.

when he could have used the deed summoning the nearest-of-kin to prove closest relationship and entitlement. Unlike others who held they did not put in a claim for they could not afford the cost, the M'Gillivrays of Harris had the means.

We can apply traditional naming patterns in the Highlands to try and identify the grandparents of the Harris family. These grandparents would have been born between 1695 and 1735, M'Gillivray grandfathers may have been named John or William, and grandmothers Mary or Marjory[91], and a brother named Roderick in either family. No Roderick M'Gillivray appears in 18th century Strathnairn, so it is more likely the name of a maternal uncle. Roderick is a traditional name for Murchisons, MacLeods, MacNeills and of course Mackenzies, the name of John Lachlan's mother.

John Lachlan's mother was the only Mrs. M'Gillivray we know of who had a brother named Roderick. Joanna was one of Alexander Mackenzie of Fairburn and Barbara Gordon's five children; a son Roderick and four daughters, namely Mary, who seems to have died unmarried in 1829 and is buried in Inverness Chapel Yard, Marjory who married Thomas Walcot and died in February 1825, Joanna who married Captain William M'Gillivray, and Isobel who married Charles Graham, merchant in London.[92] Brother Roderick (born circa 1745) married Katherine Baillie of Rosehall in 1768 and when he died six years later, there were already six children: Alexander, William, Mary, Barbara (married Kenneth Murchison), Jannet and Catherine. These were John Lachlan's cousins, some of whom appear in his will.[93] His mother though was not the only Mackenzie connection, his wife Jane Walcot was also Marjory Mackenzie's step-daughter.

Returning to the names of possible grandparents, a William and Mary M'Gillivray were Donald Roy in Balnagaig's parents. The

---

[91] Marcelle is a short form.

[92] Graham genealogies show that Isobel was a Mackenzie of Fairburn, but it is not certain she is in this position. Her children were born between 1780 and 1795.

[93] Katherine Baillie married secondly in 1777 Alexander Campbell of Delnies, sheriff-substitute of Inverness-shire, godfather to Campbell M'Intosh also of Delnies and future sheriff of Inverness. (A Jean M'Gillivray was Campbell's godmother). Katherine was widowed a second time and married lastly in 1789 William Scott of Seabank.

young Harris islanders are not his children as Donald's son William was now in Canada, but they could have been the children of a brother or sister of his; the only brother we know of is Duncan Roy.

This closing-in on grandparents' names would be totally off-target if the Harris islanders were a fragment of a larger family, if there were siblings who had not survived, or if they were an illegitimate but well-off second family.

Whatever their ancestry, these Harris M'Gillivrays, living as exiles in a beautiful but remote island, far from Dunmaglass, are members of John Lachlan M'Gillivray of Dunmaglass' 'hidden family'.

Substitution

How would the Captain Ban's line have allowed another to take over Dunmaglass, if this was the case? Perhaps all the sons were killed at Culloden, or if some members were too young to fight, died in the massacres that followed, and only one child, Lucy, survived. Yet it seems probable, given his inclusion in the Farr genealogies, that William also survived and this was known to Simon Fraser Mackintosh. Was this William in Balnagaig, or a William in Nairn? Or perhaps the Captain Ban's sons were bought out or forced to relinquish their rights.

Dunmaglass was included in the estates forfeited in 1746 by the Act of Attainder. We are led to understand that M'Intosh of Holm used canny legal arguments that succeeded. There was great obfuscation after the battle. Had the family of the man who led the most active regiment at the battle really escaped major retribution; could another line of M'Gillivrays have replaced a persistently Jacobite family? The offer of forfeited estates to different branches occurred in other clans. History gives us only the names of those who refused, such as the Macphersons and the estates of Cluny. Those who accepted would have done so as covertly as possible, to avoid the dishonour they did their chief, or alternatively to keep the estate within the clan. Genealogies would have been bent in consequence. After all, it had been an age-old tradition that clans chose their chief rather than accept the chief's son.

A take-over or substitution would not have been an isolated affair. It was about this time that Donald Roy's brother-in-law, Simon McTavish, founder of the North West Company and the wealthiest man in Canada, was taking steps to replace McTavish of Dunardry, who in 1785 was so deep in debt that he had no alternative than to sell his inheritance and work in a tax office in Edinburgh. There were secret negotiations between the two McTavishes; Dunardry did not use ordinary mail but sent a letter by a trusted friend, Duncan Campbell, to deliver personally to Simon in Canada in 1796. Not finding Simon in Montreal, Campbell waited for his arrival until the autumn, for he thought it wiser that no-one in the office should know of the contents of the letter. Such was the bashful or covert atmosphere surrounding pedigree and social status.

We cannot rule out a take-over in a different direction, for example, a Dunmaglass son in another position. All these considerations are speculative. We have laid out the facts that readers may judge for themselves.

Other claimants, other doubts

A document entitled 'The inventories of John Lachlan's miscellaneous deeds and papers not included in former Inventories found in the repositiories' was drawn up in February 1852.

Next to the listing of the Curatory act, 17 March 1797, an unknown hand has written 'N.B. This Decreet is very important as showing that the parties called to attend to the minor's interests in the appointment of Curators were Alexander M'Gillivray in Ballindruan and Jean M'Gillivray, spouse of John More M'Gillivray in Balnagaick of Dunmaglass, two of the nearest of kin to the minors on the father's side and Mrs. Marjory Mackenzie, spouse to Captain Thomas Walcot, residing in Inverness, and Mrs. Barbara Mackenzie, relict of the deceased Kenneth Murchison Esq. of Tarradale, two of the nearest in kin to the minor on the mother's side.' Questions then had arisen concerning the identities of John Lachlan's relations immediately after his death.

Clan historian, Robert MacGillivray, writes: 'I have long thought the key (to finding a chief) is the altered stone at Dunlichity, but how can it be used when we don't know what was originally on it? I believe that Angus of Dundee who claimed to be chief thought it was common knowledge in the 1920s that the real heir was bypassed because he couldn't afford to contest the chiefship – if indeed it was known in the 1850s who that should be. Nan M'Gillivray and her sisters, who ran a tartan shop in the Arcade in Inverness often told us in the 1950s/60s that her brother Jimmy was the real chief. (…) Locally there was strong feeling, which we encountered some years ago, that there were closer clansmen than the two main contestants. But there is no evidence that I am aware of. Was it suppressed – or simply not sought – by the lawyers at the time?'[94]

The 'altered stone' is a much-weathered 18th century flat stone with a missing portion: an overlying marble slab covers the gap. It is one of only three stones at Dunlichity that are carved with M'Gillivray arms, and reads: 'This in memory of (missing portion filled with marble slab) Lagg of Dun M'Glass and his spouse Margaret M'Gillivray who dyed Feb. 8 1761.' The overlying marble carries this inscription: 'Mary Gollan died at Little Mills 15.12.1868, husband Duncan M'Gillivray, died Aberarder 3.1.1894 sons Alexander and William M'Gillivray.' This is simply a duplicate of another more conventional memorial to Mary Gollan nearby.

Dr. Angus Macgillivray, Fellow of the Royal College of Medicine, in the mid 20th century claimed that the Lagg grave was that of his ancestor Finlay, a son of Dunmaglass.

There are similar arms on a second grave, with an inscription that reads: 'In memory of Murdoch Shaw, tacksman in Gask…and Anna M'Gillivray, his spouse, who died 3 November 1760, aged 39 years.' Murdoch Shaw's name appears in the list of those who were taken prisoner at the battle of Culloden, when he is described as a servant to M'Gillivray of Dunmaglass.

The third coat of arms is on the stone erected to 'Alexander, Laird of Knock Na Gail.' All these arms are very similar showing in different quarters a wild-cat ('a cat-a-mountain, sejant erect guardant'), an upheld hand ('a dexter hand gloved appaume'), a fish

---

[94] Personal correspondence

('a salmon naiant') and fourthly, a galley ('flagged, oars in saltire'). We know the ancestry of Alexander of Knocknagail, but it seems certain that both Finlay and Anna were also members of the chief's family, although they are not mentioned and there is no room for them in the traditional genealogies.[95]

In an early *Clan Chattan Journal*, there is a mention of a family of early New World settlers, scions of Dunmaglass, who lived on the banks of the river Potomac. How they were connected to Dunmaglass was not explained. One George M'Gillivray who, according to descendants, was also of the Dunmaglass family, emigrated to Canada, but from Montreal headed to Vermont and then to Whitby in 1830. He named his home Clovendale (an Anglicised version of Dalscoilt, Donald Roy's later farm) and his farm Burnside. He and siblings John, Alexander, Margaret and Ellen were children of a John M'Gillivray, lawyer in Peterhead, Aberdeen, in turn son of a William M'Gillivray and Catherine Macpherson. George and his family were treated with much deference and were well-liked in the small community where they settled.

A Cawdor and Macpherson connection

As well as the Macarthurs at Achneim, there were two other families in Cawdor who claimed relationship to the Dunmaglass M'Gillivrays. James Macpherson (1746-1834), factor to the Earl of Cawdor, wrote to his son Duncan on 15 July 1805: 'Our relation M'Gillivray of Dunmaglass is to be married to a Miss Walcot.' Although James had an illustrious descent, outside the scope of this account, we do not know his ancestry further back than his father, Neil Macpherson (1713-1795) from Tirfogrian on Lord Cawdor's estate and his mother, Jean McAndrew from Dulcie in Ardclach. Perhaps James was a great grandson of Margaret of Dunmaglass who was born in the 17th century and married a Macpherson, although such a connection is rather remote to warrant the reference.

---

[95] This or a different Finlay, a son of 'Captain Robert' (in Dalzeil), is claimed by the High Heskett Macgillivrays in Burke's Landed Gentry, 1952

A closer connection was John M'Gillivray from Dalarossie who married James' sister Ann in 1768. Ann was known as 'Lady Keppernach' after the farm they lived on in Ardclach. Nothing is known about John's relatives, although it is improbable that James would refer to them as his own.

The second family at Cawdor who claimed relationship to Dunmaglass, through a female named perhaps Margaret, and perhaps through a Macpherson ancestor rather than a M'Gillivray, held they put in a claim for Dunmaglass that had to be dropped for want of proof. There is no record of such a claim. These were the M'Gillivrays who had held the farm of Reriach in the 18th century under the alias M'Farquhar in the parish records or M'Kerchar in the rent rolls. This patronym was used by Alexander, son of Farquhar M'Allister of Dunmaglass. Together with both John Macarthur and Janet M'Gillivray, Jean's daughter at Achneim, Duncan M'Farquhar was godfather to children of a Fraser relative born in Cawdor in the 1790s. His son John, merchant, married to Margaret Macarthur, was reportedly a 'claimant' at the litigation.

Curiosity

Going through deeds and documents, we see that the history of the M'Gillivrays often mystified researchers in the past: wills, gravestones and parish records have been manipulated or annotated. Entries in some of the registers relating to M'Gillivrays bear pencil marks and crosses. Even a few graves at Dunlichity look forced open in some ghoulish exercise.

Had the parish registers for Daviot & Dunlichity covering the 18th century survived, there would have been fewer, if any, questions. The register for Boleskine fell in to a fast-flowing river, and the registers for Daviot & Dunlichity that were kept at the parish school apparently burnt in a fire. Reverend Alexander Gordon wrote in the *First Statistical Account* in the 1790s that no births or marriages were recorded in the past four years 'due to an incident'. A later parish register that starts in the 1770s is very badly kept. There were no marriages entered between 1780 and 1804; some later marriages carry only one name; there are pages crossed out, numerous insertions and a general lack of chronology. But the most curious page carries only two large inkspills and additions of sums of money, together with the signature of Charles M'Intosh. Charles M'Intosh was the name of Colonel John's lawyer (and later the laird of M'Intosh's). Why was Charles M'Intosh totting up sums in the parish register and why was it in his possession?

There are anomalies concerning M'Gillivrays in other parish registers as well. The Cawdor register, as we have seen, has been vandalised for marriages that may have told us something about Janet who married John Macarthur. In the Nairn register, there is an insertion in large handwriting that does not belong to the usual scribe. On 9 May 1742, the baptism of a child called William, to William M'Gillivray in town. The entry sports a huge smudge. Like all curiosities in the registers involving M'Gillivrays, it may be claim-related. Was this the William of Simon Fraser Mackintosh's genealogies, a son of William, the Captain Ban? Could he have been a brother to Donald Roy at Balnagaig?[96]

So we can spend many hours leafing through registers and deeds, wondering who the Dunmaglass M'Gillivrays really were, and we wouldn't be the first. In the 19th century, an anonymous enquirer wrote to *Scottish Notes & Queries* on 21 February 1867.[97]

---

[96] Inverness merchant Charles M'Gillivray declared bankruptcy in 1806 despite an earlier bank facility for £200 guaranteed by Donald M'Gillivray of Dalcroilt (father of William of the North West Company), Reverend Roderick Mackenzie of Knockbain and Angus Macdonald (probably William's brother-in-law). Reverend Roderick ('Parson Rory') was a surprising financier. He was a man of 'unbounded charity, very benevolent and particularly attentive to the poor and destitute. He was upwards of six feet in height, with broad shoulders and massive well-proportioned limbs and universally allowed to be one of the finest-looking Highlanders of his day'. In 1783 he married Mary, sister of Charles Grant, Member of Parliament and father of Lord Glenelg. If not connected to John Lachlan's mother, Joanna McKenzie, Roderick was connected to the M'Gillivrays of Aldourie through his wife's brother. Charles was not a common name for a M'Gillivray at the time. There are none recorded in the 18th century in the parish registers for Inverness and only one in Nairn born in 1743. It is interesting to note a Charles, the name of one of the Captain Ban's sons, in the company of Donald Roy. Marjory Wilkins Campbell, William M'Gillivray's biographer, writes that Donald Roy had six daughters and six sons but did not name them all.

[97] A regular and erudite contributor to the magazine at the time was Reverend Mackenzie Walcot (1821-1880), one time curator of St Margaret's, Westminster, and author of numerous church histories. His knowledge was extensive and he enjoyed discussing the arcane, such as the species of fish in the Merry Wives of Windsor. When Walcot himself put a query, it was to ask about the genealogy of the Walcots of Tipperary. Reverend Walcot's father, an only son, was cousin of John Lachlan's wife, whose step-mother was

'Enclosed I beg to hand you an extract from *the Gentleman's Magazine,* and if not trespassing too much on your valuable space, beg to request the insertion of a few Queries in reference thereto.

"Feb 17, at Pensacola, a Creek chief, very much lamented by those who knew him best. There happened to be at that time at Pensacola a numerous band of Creeks, who watched his illness with the most marked anxiety, and when his death was announced to them, and while they followed him to the grave, it is impossible for words to describe the loud screams of real woe which they vented in their unaffected grief. He was by his father's side a Scotchman of the respectable family of Drumnaglass in Inverness-shire. The vigour of his mind overcame the disadvantages of an education had in the wilds of America, and he was well acquainted with all the most useful European sciences. In the latter part of his life he composed with great care the history of several classes of the original inhabitants of America; and this he intended to present to Professor Robertson for publication in the next edition of his History. The American and European writer are now no more, and the MSS of the latter, it is feared, have perished for the Indians adhere to their custom of destroying whatever inanimate objects a dead friend most delighted in. It is only since Mr. M'Gillivray had influence amongst them that they have suffered the slaves of a deceased master to live." *Gentleman's Magazine, vol lxiii, p 767, 1793.*

1. Can I find any more detailed account of the life and family of this Mr. M'Gillivray?

2. Are his MSS destroyed, as represented in the Gent. Mag, or are they still in existence? If so, where can they be seen?

3. What arms do the Drumnaglass family bear?

Marjory Mackenzie. This is the only known connection of the Walcots with the Mackenzies, although Mackenzie Walcot was born in Bath, at the same time as the Mackenzies and Murchisons in our story lived at nearby Bathampton.

This and any other information on the subject will be greatly esteemed by AKM, Princes Street, Cavendish Square'

We wonder who ADM was and how much he knew about the Dunmaglass family. There don't seem to have been any replies. The arms question is significant in Victorian Britain – arms guaranteed descent. Unlike Findlay, Anna and the Knocknagael's stones, there are no arms on the graves of the children of William of Dunmaglass, Barbara Ann and John Lachlan.

Dunlichity

The M'Gillivray story is a jigsaw puzzle with missing pieces, or a chess game where we don't see all of the moves taking place. To increase our confusion, the rules of the game might not apply: we do not know what is true and what is not. There are very few family papers that have survived and even fewer testimonies from outsiders. The whereabouts of the original documents that were printed for the litigation are not known, the book of genealogies in the possession of the last Dalcrombie is lost, and documents that Charles Fraser Mackintosh had access to when writing his account of the family are untraceable.

The people are as enigmatic as the places where they worshipped and lived. Of the latter, Robert and George M'Gillivray, authors of the Clan book, were moved to write:

'Dunmaglass! No other name is so evocative or so meaningful to MacGillivrays. A name redolent with romanticism, embodying the whole tradition of the Race, whose soft Gaelic cadence is capable of bewitching the heart and soothing the soul. Yet a name to inspire, to conjure up the spirit of long dead heroes….a name as mysterious in its sibilance as in its interpretation.'

The sacred lands where the M'Gillivrays worshipped and were buried are at Dunlichity, in a secluded Highland glen. Two previous churches were on the site of the existing one, built in 1759. A church inspector, surrounded by his parishioners for safety, came here after the first Jacobite rebellion to investigate complaints against Mister Michael, the painting minister. The former wrote:

'With some difficulty I gott acess to the church, and had no sooner begun worshipe than by stones thrown in, the pulpit was broke about me, and some of my parishioners wounded. Being obliged to remove for our safety, we were assaulted by a multitude of men and women, with swords, staves and stones, some of our number wounded, and others barbarously beaten.'

But fortunately religious fervour has here subsided, life in the Highlands is changed. The iron chain clanks in the fresh mountain air as you push the gates open, then there is silence and you are alone with the past. A rich green sloping hillside surrounds the walled enclosure built for some of the Dunmaglass families of this story: Farquhar of Dalcrombie, Alexander of the Carolinas and Knocknagael, his wife Anne Fraser, Barbara Ann and John Lachlan, children of Captain William. The grandest monument is to Donald Roy M'Gillivray and his wife Ann M'Tavish. Alexander, hero of Culloden, is buried near the sea at the Church of Petty. There is a second enclosure for the Shaws of Tordarroch. All around, closer to the church, are ancient and recent graves of Dunlichity parishioners. There is an unusual watch-tower in the walls built in the early 19th century to ward off the body-snatchers and grave-stealers of the times, although that the latter should show interest in a poor and remote Highland graveyard is hard to believe.

The kirk and its churchyard have the unusual feature of being built like the galley on the old M'Gillivray coats of arms: its bow is pitched westward up a hill, the Scotch firs drop their branches over the grass decks that are the burial grounds, like so much surf spilling from the seas it cuts through on its onward path.

Many M'Gillivrays in this history, and others, unnamed, who should be in it, are buried here, even though there are no gravestones to mark their final resting places. There is no stone for Lachlan, the wealthy benefactor of Dunmaglass, who at his death filled this church as no-one else had ever done, no stones for his sister Jean and her husband Duncan Roy, nor for the rich Colonel John who aspired to possess all these lands. We admonish John Lachlan for omitting to erect monuments in memory of such august patrons. The imposing gravestones in the enclosure are all the more disquieting when those that should be here are not.

The congregation no longer has any M'Gillivrays. An illustrious member in the not so distant past was the late Duke of Gloucester, born in 1901. He stayed on his visits to his rented estates at the old house of Farr, where Simon Fraser Mackintosh wrote his genealogies with the help of his M'Gillivray mother. The former Grand Prior of the Order of the Hospital of St John of Jerusalem, spiritual heirs of the old Knights Templars whose lands encompassed Lonnie and Dalzeil, sat with his family in an ordinary pew in the congregation. One of the Duke's titles was Baron Culloden, and if he could hear ghosts, he would have listened to the voices of the Jacobite clans of the past, who were here exhorted by Mister Michael to take up arms against this visitor's Hanoverian ancestors and fight for the king of Scotland.

To the Highlander, the voices whisper something else: 'Look at this galley of your ancestors! See it from the bow as it goes westward, to the lochs, the seas, the setting sun. Look back to the holy captain's bridge and below the decks to those with the oars, who take you onwards with their blood, their labour and their tears. It is we who move the galley that gives you passage – the ancestors of this small Highland family.'

APPENDIX

Letter from Lachlan to Jean Roy[98]

NATIONAL ARCHIVES OF SCOTLAND GD128/23/5/18

Inverness, 16 August 1772

Dear Sister,

I have given a letter to our cousin Dalcrombie wherein I desire him to provide you so early as the season will permit, cow milck, cow, six four year old, young cows, one young work horse, twenty four sheep, and a ram and a young bull if you should have occasion for it. I hope this will be a sufficient stocking for your farm at least, for the present. Now Sister, I can if you and your worthy husband consider the expense and concern I take for you and family, you will certainly allow that I have a right to expect your utmost diligence and care of what I put in your hands. Go assured that I have no pleasure in throwing away money to no purpose and when that is the case, I will be tired and induced to slack my hand; on the contrary, when you convince me and the world that you manage your farm and cattle to the best advantage it will be an encouragement to me to do the more for you. I am told your worthy husband thinks himself too much of a gentleman to put up the sheep when you are not at home, and that once in particular, when you were at the house of Dunmaglass one evening, Duncan and his man would not put up the sheep but obliged you after coming home to go to the hill for them, what can I think of such a despicable, worthless wretch as that; it is truly provoking. I wish I could speak to him, but you may tell him from me, if

---

[98] Lachlan's success and prestige in America were based on his discretion and diplomacy; this letter reflects nothing of these characteristics. Although we find this letter suspect, Lachlan may have treated women callously, for by leaving America to return to Scotland he is accused of abandoning his Creek wife and children with no means of support.

he does not use his utmost industry and care in managing the stocking, I will certainly turn him out of the place and let him get bread where he will. As for the farm, I think he has no business to meddle with it, and it is my desire that he shall not direct nor interfere with the man who may be interested in the management of it, but if he continues in his obstinacy and will not sit the part he is desired and (illegible), he will have cause to repent it, when it will be too late to mind. He may assure himself that I will be as good as my word. I wish you health, I am, Your affectionate Brother, Lachlan M'Gillivray

PS I shall keep the task of Ballanagacek in my own hands until I see matters mang'd in some (illegible) to satisfaction for I find that you are weak and silly to let that husband of yours do what he pleases. It shows your want of spirit, or you would not suffer it to be.

There are four more lines to this letter, which are incomprehensible because parts of the page are torn and missing.

Handwritten on letter: Mr. Lachlan M'Gillivray, Dunmaglass to his sister Jean, lamenting the doings of her husband Duncan 16.8.1772

Bishop Forbes

Robert Forbes, Bishop of Ross and Caithness 1746-1775, was so appalled by the behaviour of the Duke of Cumberland after Culloden that he devoted the remainder of his life to collecting testimonies of the atrocities committed. His collection of journals, narratives and memoranda relating to the life of Prince Charles Edward Stuart, during and after the 1745 rising, was published as *The Lyon in Mourning*. He also kept diaries of two visits to Episcopal congregations in the north of Scotland. The extract below is from his second visit in 1770 to Strathnairn, the same year Lachlan arrived from America.

It was 6 June, and Bishop Forbes was on his way to Inverness on the road built by General Wade in the aftermath of the first rebellion in 1715.[99] General Oughton, Grand master of the Scottish freemasons, was also making his way to Inverness, but was taken ill and had inconveniently taken all the beds at the king's house in Aviemore for the night, so Forbes had to press on to M'Gillivray's Inn at Dalmagarry. The inn had formerly been held by Gillies M'Bean, another Culloden hero; the present innkeeper was William M'Gillivray, farmer, most likely the former schoolmaster at Cawdor, now elder of the church of Moy.

The following night Forbes was able to 'set up' at the Horns in Inverness, where General Oughton was meeting with the town's freemasons. Although in Inverness to review Fort George for the first time, he was now being asked to have Robert Warrand, the powerful and abusive postmaster of Inverness, removed from his post. (The most salacious crime Warrand was accused of was opening and passing on the love letters of Thomas Walcot, future father-in-law of John Lachlan, when he was courting his first wife Betsy Fraser.) Two nights previously, there had been a Freemason's meeting at St Andrew's Kilwinning to draw up a petition to the Grand Master. Although a full meeting, it was sparsely attended: Captain William M'Gillivray of Dunmaglass, William Inglis of Kingsmills, merchant and future provost, Captain Shaw of Tordarroch, Bailie John M'Intosh, Major Allan Duff, Captain Alexander Duff, and Mr. William Cuthbert. According to Inglis, at a subsequent court case brought by Warrand, the petition was signed by Captain M'Gillivray as Master and Captain Shaw and Alexander

---

[99] General Wade headed a military presence that was meant to pacify the Highlands; he built roads, barracks and fortresses and had a hard time with the Highlanders who, when they could, hindered his efforts and blocked the roads by night. The First Disarming Act had brought in few of their weapons; the second Act in 1725 gave Wade broader powers: he could search for and seize arms instead of awaiting their surrender. A special summons was published for 'all of the name of M'Intosh, and their tribes and followers, in the parishes of Dunleckity, Dores, Moy, Dallaricie, Croy and Petty, and to all others of them inhabiting the four Parish of Badenoch – vis. Inch Aby, Kinghuizie and Laggan, in the shire of Inverness, and to those of the Parish of Calder, in the Shire of Nairn' to surrender their broadswords, targets, poynards, whizars or duks, side pistol of side pistols, guns, or any other warlike weapons.'

M'Intosh as wardens.[100] One half of Inverness was fighting the other about the removal of Warrand: the masons succeeded.

From Inverness, Bishop Forbes visited Torbreck where he confirmed the ageing Fraser of Phopachie, together with Isabel M'Gillivray, a 'person of years'. On 26 June, Forbes 'communicated' with Lady Dunmaglass and her two daughters. Although Catherine and Elizabeth alone appear in the books of deeds at an early date as daughters of Lady Dunmaglass, William himself recognized another sister Anne who played a crucial role in the management of Dunmaglass during his absence. Three days later Forbes baptised 'Elizabeth Shaw, alias Mrs. M'Gillavrie of Dalcrombie, who, her husband, Farquhar M'Gillaray, Mr. Alexander Shaw, Isabel Dallas, alias Mrs. Shaw and Anne Shaw were confirmed'. Forbes wrote a detailed description of the lands of Dalcrombie, whose wildness and diversity had impressed him.

'Saturday morning, June 30. Confirmed Mrs. Grant, sister to Dalcrombie, and Margaret MacLean. Matins and Vespers in every House we lodged…left Elrigg at ½ after 12, and came to Letterwheelin, the habitation of M'Gillavrie of Dalcrombie, 20 minutes after 1. The most rugged Road this in the world, but beautifully variegated with high hills, grand rocks, deep lochs, and verdant woods, particularly one large hill of natural wood, abounding with roe and roe-buck. It was diverting to see how warily the highland garrons made their way, step by step, in a narrow sheep or goat road, sometimes stepping like dogs oer huge stones.

In this short way, we came in view of no fewer than seven lochs; the first called Loch Ruthven, two miles long, and having a particular fine species of trout; the second, like an artificial basin called Dalochan, the third called Lochcorr, the fourth called Loch Dentellchack, the fifth called Loch Ashy, the six and sevenths lochs are lesser ones – all of them abounding with trout and pyke (…).

---

[100] There is some confusion in dates here; Captain William was Master only in 1768 according to Masonic records in Inverness.

It is still remarkable, if not wonderful, that Loch Dentellchack never freezes (and yet on December 24 it was frozen over – 1773 – a thing that had never happened before, and surprised everybody) in winter, but one day's or night's frost in the spring will freeze it efectually. And which is still more surprising, a burn, issuing out of Duntellchack into an eight loch, not yet in our view, called Loch-Clachan, does not freeze but when its original fountain, Dentellchack, is frozen, and the stream of it is seen running through the middle of Loch Clachan, when Loch-Clachan itself is frozen. Let naturalists account for this, if they can, for to me it seems inexplicable. The rivulet out of Dentellchack has a forcible current through Loch-Clachan, but glides smoothly on.

Capn. M'Gillavrie of Dumnaglash met us at Letterwheelin. We were eighteen at table, dinner and supper. At Tordarroch, Ellrig and Letterwheelin – three farmer houses – we were so elegantly and even sumptuously entertained, eight, nine or ten dishes on the table, with desserts – that Rachel[101] and I could not help being surprised, insomuch that this day she spoke out and plainly declared that the meat we had on the table at dinner would not hae been purchased at Edinburgh, or Leith for a guinea. At all the three houses we had plenty of good wine, and punch, and variety of milks. Hard by Letterwheelin, a romantic situation, truly, is a large wood, being part of the farm, to which we gentlemen retired in the afternoon for a walk. Here M'Intosh of Esseck explained to me the economy of these entertainments thus. 'You and Mrs. Forbes', said he, 'are surprised at the way in which we entertain you; but we farmers in this country can easily give a dinner to a friend than gentlemen of 6 or 700 guineas a year can give one at Edinburgh or Leith, as every dish we put on the table we have in our own farms, only we must give out a little money for wine, tea and sugar. For instance, we are here at a neighbour's house, who has 40 milk cows, consequently he must have plenty of good beef and veal; and he has a great flock of sheep, consequently

---

[101] Bishop Forbes' wife and travelling companion

must have plenty of good mutton and lamb. He has likewise a numerous flock of goats, consequently plenty of goat-flesh and kid. Here we walk in a wood, where roe and roe buck bound up and down. Then in Loch Dentellchack, along the foot of the wood (pointing to it) plenty of good and large trout. Not far from this we can have salmon at command, and in the hills there is great plenty of game.' At all the three houses we saw plenty of geese, turkeys, ducks and poultry. …

We were pressingly invited to be at Dumnaglash's house, but could not accept of the kind importunity, as we resolved to set out for Argylshire.

Sunday - 3rd after Trinity - July 1, morning - Baptised and confirmed two daughters of Dalcrombie's by a former marriage.

This morning, Mr. Allan Cameron baptised Dumnaglash's Black Boy, and then went off before us to have things in readiness.

We rode along the south side of Loch Dentellchack, and cross'd a corner of it; then came to Loch Clachan, a corner of which we likewise crossed, and saw the burn running into it from Dentellchack. A very rough road this. The Black boy rode before one of the young ladies, to whom I said, 'Do you know, Miss, what you are like just now? Even like one behind a black crow, sticking firmly to the shoulders of the horse'.'

Bishop Forbes' humour is dubious. Not so his spiritual zeal. Elizabeth Shaw was clearly already confirmed, having married in church nine years previously. Anabaptism was anathema to Episcopal ministers, but Bishop Forbes re-baptised the 15-month-old brother of the future Sir James Mackintosh. We do not know how Dunmaglass acquired his Black Boy – perhaps Lachlan brought him as a gift. It was fashionable at this time to own black boy slaves; Bishop Forbes baptised two more at Fortrose. Most eventually ran away and lived in freedom in the cities.

Bishop Forbes stopped in Inverness and admired the hundred or so children employed in the M'Intosh hemp factory set up by the provost, spinning and working on the looms. They earned 4 shilling a week when 'formerly they were idle and vagrants…it is delightful to see them so diligent and cheerful at work'.

More about Reverend Lachlan

Reverend Lachlan M'Gillivray, as we have seen, was the grandson of Archibald of Charles Town and Daviot, and the son of Lachlan of Sunflower Estate, Jamaica. When Archibald died, Lachlan's sister Janet and brother Alexander were at Daviot, while James was still in Georgia. About John, who had also gone to America, there is no more information. Sir Aeneas M'Intosh, their father's first cousin, was relentlessly trying to recover the property and exerted much pressure on them with legal procedures as well as through friends and relatives. Handling their finances was Provost John M'Intosh, their mother's cousin. On one occasion Janet complained to him bitterly: 'Some brothers are very kind, and others are void of affection; and, to be plain with you, sir, this is the case with the brother I live with. From the day of my father's death to this good hour, I never received a shilling out of his hands. Did not my brother Lachlan remember me, I do not know what I should do; so that I expect to be excused for not throwing myself entirely in the power of so selfish a person.'

James eventually returned to Inverness seriously ill. Janet wrote that her brother Sandie was also in very bad health: 'The imbecility of his body and mind is every day gaining ground. I too am complaining. I find that griefe and misfortunes which has been my portion in this transitory state has undermined a naturally good constitution.' When the much-respected and ever-polite Provost expressed sympathy, Janet was touched. 'Much do we stand in need of some kind friends taking a concern, and there is none in existence whose counsel we would pay greater deference to, or rely more upon than yours.'

When their cousin Anne at Aberchalder died in 1801 or 1802 there was some financial relief, for she left Alexander a quarter of her estate, which comprised her part of the sale of Aberchalder. By the winter of 1806, James was dead, Sandy was still in bad health and the laird of M'Intosh was pressing hard for the M'Gillivrays to vacate Daviot. But Janet would have been reassured since Lachlan had returned from Jamaica and after a stay in London was on his way to Inverness. The first thing Lachlan saw to on arrival was the renunciation of Daviot to the Laird of M'Intosh. It was a lengthy procedure: Provost John M'Intosh had a sasine or mortgage on the lands for money lent to Archibald in 1778. Although the matter of Daviot was finalised in 1811, Janet was still living there in 1816.

Not long after arriving in Inverness, on Christmas day 1807, 50-year old Lachlan married the eldest daughter of Inverness doctor and freemason William Kennedy and wife Mary Randal Scott, the childhood love of Sir James Mackintosh. Ann McKenzie Kennedy was barely seventeen. Dr. Kennedy could only have agreed to his young daughter's marriage with an ageing and 'rheumaticky' Jamaican planter for want of a more suitable young suitor; the young men were leaving Scotland in search of fortunes abroad. Lachlan was also the father of children from a first liaison in the West Indies, but given the dazzle of Jamaican fortunes and the general frugality of Inverness, this was probably no obstacle. The circumstances of Lachlan, owner of a sugar plantation, slaves and a good herd of cattle, may have appeared better than they really were. Ann's younger more wilful sister, 'bonnie' Mary Randal Jean, was to set tongues wagging when she eloped three years later with a young soldier of good fortune, Chessborough Grant Falconer, brother to a recent First Secretary of the Madras Presidency, then stationed at Fort William with his regiment.

At their marriage, Lachlan settled his assets on his wife. They had four children, two of whom survived: Lachlan born in 1808 and Mary Randal a few years later. Lachlan returned to the West Indies when his wife was pregnant with a fourth child, either at the behest of his children there or because slave riots were jeopardising the value of Jamaican plantations. Catastrophe came in the form of collapsing sugar prices and the end of slave-importation which may have been Lachlan's economic mainstay. Before leaving Scotland, he made a will whereby his wife would have a handsome annuity and all her jewels, trinkets and ornaments. He made provision for both his lawful and two 'reputed' children, James and Janet

M'Gillivray in Jamaica. The well-intentioned financial arrangements came to nought. The following notice appeared in the *Inverness Journal and Northern Advertiser* in February 1816: 'Died on the 19th November last at Sunflower, St Thomas in the East, Jamaica, Lauchlan M'Gillivray, Esquire of Sunflower, fifth son of the late Archibald M'Gillivray, Esq. Daviot.'

Lachlan's first family is described in a letter written by an Australian-born grandson, also named Lachlan. He recounts how his planter grandfather married a daughter of Macpherson, a chieftain of the clan, and had a child James Lachlan (1800-1863). (Lachlan M'Gillivray is found with one white dependent in Black River, Jamaica in 1796.) Although this child was his Daviot aunt Janet's favourite nephew, she left her property to Lachlan's second wife 'under influence as she hated the stepmother'. The account continues:

> 'On account of this stepmother's extravagance, Lachlan had to sell Daviot and reside in his West Indian estate. Before his second marriage he was a wealthy man, having an estate in America left him by Col. M'Gillivray. His son James Lachlan took over the sugar plantation and had to fight a keen battle with the stepmother, who tried to get what was left. He was only a youth and almost friendless, but he sailed for London. He managed to take £2000-£3000 with him. He found his aunt Janet dead and his stepmother in possession. He left for Australia. In person (he) was a strongly built man, scarcely middle height, strong marked features, not unhandsome, studious habits, proud and distant and with a very bad temper...'[102]

Ann Kennedy, the 'wicked stepmother', had, according to Lachlan's earlier family, stolen an inheritance that should have been theirs.

---

[102] *Clan Chattan Journal.* James Lachlan had arrived in Australia from Scotland in 1822, as a cabin passenger on the 'Deveron'. At the Scots Church in Sydney in 1830, he married Jane Bradley, a ward of Reverend Dunmore Lang, founder of the Presbyterian Church in Australia. One of his Australian great-granddaughters corresponded with Aeneas Lionel M'Intosh, who accompanied Shackleton on the 1907 and 1914 expeditions to Antarctica. Aeneas was grandson of the Aeneas M'Intosh born in Canada who would testify in favour of Neil John M'Gillivray at the litigation. The younger Aeneas apparently knew the M'Gillivray family well although it is not known how.

There is no record of Colonel John leaving an estate to Lachlan in America, although he had abandoned a tract of land 'Sunflowers' near Mobile in 1780, next to land belonging to Lachlan's maternal uncle, James M'Intosh of Kyllachy, who would disinherit Lachlan and his siblings.

Besides the ornaments, trinkets, linen and jewels that Lachlan bequeathed to his young wife, it is uncertain whether there was much more to leave, for the Jamaican estate seems to have gone to his first family. Two or three years after Lachlan's death, his sister died in May 1818 in Inverness. She left the little she had to her young nephew and niece, Lachlan and Mary Randal. Their mother Ann was her executrix, and Dalcrombie's daughter Janet and husband Michael handled the funeral arrangements. Despite this small inheritance, money was in short supply and Ann and her children returned to the parental home. When her father died in early 1823, her mother again found herself in distressed circumstances.

Her old beau, James Mackintosh, now a renowned politician in London, flew to their rescue. With his cousin, the younger Charles Grant, MP for Inverness-shire, he visited the Prime Minister to plead for Mary Kennedy, 'widow of an Inverness doctor and Mackintosh's intimate friend from childhood'. Their memorandum stated:

> 'Her husband who had originally served in medical offices in the Army and was for thirty years the principal physician at Inverness where he lately died and from his disinterestedness and generosity has left his widow with little provision for three children and two grandchildren. Almost all those who could now have supplied the place of a husband to her have fallen in the service of their country. Major Scott her brother was killed at Albuera. One of her sons was killed at Waterloo. Major-General Mackenzie, her nearest relation, was killed at Talavera.'

Lord Liverpool granted a pension of £100.[103]

---

[103] Patrick O'Leary. *Sir James Mackintosh, The Whig Cicero*

One of the two grandchildren was of course the future Reverend Lachlan, who is first found in a minor civil servant position in the antipodes, then as a church minister and finally a New Zealand Member of Parliament. Robert McGillivray, clan historian, has traced his life and movements. The first record of him is in 1832 when he had been in Van Diemen's Land or Tasmania as Assistant Corresponding clerk for nine months at a salary of £80 per annum. A document in Tasmanian archives shows that he found his salary inadequate and asked for a rise of £40, which he soon obtained as second Paper Clerk. A few months later he resigned, declaring that he 'had been required to write précis and for this extra duty he had received no additional remuneration'.

Lachlan may have had his next assignment already lined up; this was to accompany Dunmore Lang of the Scots Kirk on a visit to Britain to chose and bring back some ninety emigrants. Dr. Lang tried to get Lachlan involved in a further venture for skilled emigrants from Scotland in 1836: 'I could get a young gentleman who has already had great experience in this matter to accompany me home and superintend the details. This gentleman is Mr. L. M'Gillivray, a relative of the late Sir James Macintosh.[104] He was my fellow passenger to and from England in 1833 and 1834 and selected the emigrants for the 'James'. He is particularly well acquainted with the Highlands of Scotland, the best place perhaps for obtaining shepherds; and being himself of a highly respectable family from that part of the kingdom, he would have much more weight than a stranger. I am sure two hundred pounds per annum, with travelling expenses, would satisfy him.'

Nothing came of Lang's proposal.[105] A second attempt at finding Lachlan a job was made by a Tasmanian farmer from Nairn, James Grant, in a letter to the governor of the island, who was acquainted with the Falconer uncle who had many years previously eloped with bonnie Miss Kennedy. Grant wrote that he himself had known Mrs. M'Gillivray and Mrs. Falconer in Scotland in his youth

---

[104] Firstly their M'Gillivray grandfathers were brothers; secondly Sir James' father was brother of Lachlan's grandmother Lucy M'Intosh.

[105] The years of the first visit to England do not tally with the date of a letter (10 January 1834) in which James Grant, formerly of Nairn and now living in Tasmania, stated that Lachlan was with him; this was perhaps due to a scribal error.

when they had attended the same school. Lachlan was now seeking a position. 'He is well-educated and informed – steady and most serious in his habits and as a missionary would, I think, be enthusiastic in the cause of religion and reformation – his means are limited.' In April 1836 Lachlan conducted services at Grant's estate for the men employed there but was still after a government appointment, which he eventually obtained for £50 per annum, less than the earlier salary he deemed inadequate.

In 1839, Lachlan returned to Britain and the following spring married Catherine Anne Sloane of Peebles. The couple returned to Van Diemen's Land where two daughters were born. He spent a few years farming until he was appointed inspector of Stock and catechist 'taking Divine Service according to the Church of England'. He was again looking for better employment and petitioned the Comptroller-General of Convicts. The latter noted he had a recommendation from the Colonial Secretary Lord Glenelg and appointed him schoolmaster to Wesbury Probation Station.[106] At about this time, Lachlan's sister Mary Randall, in her mid-thirties and living in Dover, married Anthony Cuthbert Collingwood Denny, grandson and heir to Admiral Lord Collingwood who fought with Lord Nelson at Trafalgar.

In 1847 the Free Presbyterian Church of Victoria appointed Lachlan minister near Ballarat. He resigned three months later because the church required too much regarding 'trials for his licence', which he considered an indignity given he had studied theology for fifteen years and preached for four. The United Presbyterian Church of Victoria was less exacting and ordained him minister in Melbourne, then Belfast and lastly, in 1849, Warrnambool where he remained four years, his longest stay in one post. When a son was born here, he named him John Lachlan, presumably after the childless Dunmaglass, although even if aware of the existence of his namesake and the aspirations of the father, John Lachlan did not remember him in his will.

When news came of Dunmaglass' death, Lachlan and his family packed their bags and returned to Scotland. It was a restless minister, dissatisfied with his various opportunities, who took

---

[106] Lord Glenelg's mother was a Fraser of Balnain.

lodgings in Academy Street close to where John Lachlan died and where a daughter, Anna Jane Elizabeth, was born. Here he prepared his claim for Dunmaglass as nearest heir-male.

The fairy tale whose hero is William, the Captain Ban, as told by Simon Fraser Mackintosh

FARR MANUSCRIPT IN NATIONAL LIBRARY OF SCOTLAND, EDINBURGH

About the beginning of the 18th century the wife of one of the tenants in Druim-a-ghadna, upon the estate of Dunmaglass, had been carried away by the fairies, and was said to have been taken by them into a small hillock in that neighbourhood called 'Tomnashangan', or the Ants Hill, and had been absent from her family for nearly a year. No person, however, could tell exactly where she was, although their suspicions fell upon the fairies, and that she must be with them in the hill now mentioned. Several attempts were made to discover her, and none were bold enough to encounter the residence of the fairires. At last Captain William M'Gillivray, alias the 'Captain Ban', ie 'White', son of Farquhar M'Gillivray of Dunmaglass, who was resident at the spot, volunteered his services to endeavour to get the woman released from her long captivity in the 'Fairy Hill' if it was possible that she could be there. The Captain being informed that John Duh (M'Chuile) Macqueen of Pollachaik was familiar and on good terms with the fairies, and that he had wax candles in which there was a particular virtue, he despatched a messenger to the far-famed Pollachaik for one of his candles in order to assist him in discovering the lost female. The candle was given by Pollachaik to the messenger, who got particular instructions never to look behind him until he reached home, otherwise something might happen to him, and he would lose the candle. This person heard so much noise like that of horses and carriages, accompanied with music and loud cries of 'Catch him, catch him' at Craignuan, near Moyhall, that he was so frightened that he could not help looking behind him, and although he saw nothing, he lost the candle, then he made the best of his way home.

A second courier was despatched, who received another candle, and the same instructions. In coming through the same place as the former, he withstood all the noise he heard there, but at a place near Farr it was ten times worse, and, not being able to withstand taking a peep over his shoulder, he lost the object of his message. In this predicament, it became necessary to send a third bearer to Pollachaik for another candle, which he also got, but on coming to the River Findhorn, it was so large that he could not cross, so that he was obliged to go back to the Laird for his advice, who, upon coming down to the bank of the river, desired the man to throw a stone upon the opposite side of the river, and no sooner was this done than much to his astonishment he found himself also there. He then proceeded upon his journey, and having taken a different route across the hills, even here he occasionally heard considerable noise, but he had the courage never to look behind him, and accordingly he put the virtued candle into the hands of Captain Ban.

The Captain being now possessed of Pollochaik's wee candle, he one evening approached the hillock, and having discovered where the entry was, entered the passage to the fairy habitation, and passing a press in the entrance, it is said that the candle immediately lighted of its own accord, and he discovered that the good lady, the object of his mission, was busily engaged in a reel, and the whole party singing and dancing, and dressed in neat green jackets, bedgowns, &c. The Captain took her out of one of the reels, and upon obtaining the open air, he told her how very unhappy her husband and friends were at the length of time she had been absent from them, but the woman had been so enchanted and encaptured with the society she had been in, that she seemed to think she had been only absent one night, instead of a year, from her house. When the Captain brought her off with him, the fairies were so enraged that they said 'they would keep him in view'. The woman was brought to her disconsolate husband, and the candle was faithfully preserved in the family for successive generations in order to keep off all fairies, witches, brownies and water-kelpies in all time to come.

Some time afterwards, as the Captain was riding home at night by the west end of Lochduntelchaig, he was attacked and severely beaten by some people he could not recognise. He got home to his own house, but never recovered, and it is said that the mare he rode was worse to him than even those that attacked him; so he ordered her to be shot the following day. He was granduncle to the present John Lachlan M'Gillivray of Dunmaglass.

The third and successful bearer of the candle was Archibald M'Gillivray in (blank), alias 'Gillespie Luath', ie Swift or fast Archibald. He was granduncle to Archibald M'Gillivray, now tenant in Dunmaglass. Pollochaik said to him that he would have preferred the Captain to have sent for his fold of cattle than for the candle.

The candle was in possession of some of her descendants about thirty years ago, but was afterwards taken away by some idle boys. The woman lived to such an old age that some of the people still in life (1835) remember quite well having seen her shearing the corn upon her knees, in consequence of having lost the use of her lower limbs.

I was drawn into researching the Dunmaglass litigation when my father's sister Marjory died in South Africa in 1996. She was a keen and brave genealogist of the old school, spending her holidays in Scotland scraping back moss from gravestones to find names that might shed light on a family mystery. On one of her father John Walker Macgillivray ('Jack')'s visits to Britain in his youth, an uncle in London told him he remembered that the family had put in a claim for Dunmaglass. When Jack retired from the Colonial service many years later, he tried to contact relatives in Cawdor. John, merchant, replied to his letter; he remembered Jack's father visiting at the turn of the century, taking the family for a drive in the countryside, an unforgettable event in those early days of motorcars. John firmly confirmed what Jack's uncle had told him; his own father too had often said that Dunmaglass should have been theirs. The details though were unclear as in any family legend. The family, it was remembered, had been claimants, had 'lost' on account of a missing link and were involved by descent from a daughter of the Dunmaglass family whose name may have been Margaret.

When I inherited Marjory's papers, the internet age was dawning and research no longer restricted to deciphering old tombstones. Direct communication and exchange of information between M'Gillivrays all over the world had become possible. I attended a clan gathering in Inverness in 1997 that was a walk down clan memory lane. However, there was a dearth of genealogical information. I had not yet met Roy M'Gilvray in Canada, whose endeavours to sort out the M'Gillivrays constitute an opus mirabile.

My grandfather Jack was born in Tobago, was Crown Surveyor in Trinidad and died in London in 1961. His father was Duncan who with his bride Elizabeth Walker, daughter of an Auldearn farmer, left the peaceful village of Cawdor where his father was postmaster and general merchant. Eliza was born and raised at Brightmoney, the Brodie's dower house; her family were Hamilton Souter and William Barclay's closest neighbours. Many of Duncan's family had left, for Edinburgh, London and Canada, where with industry and ability they found a better life than they could have expected in their village. In Tobago, Duncan worked for the main exporters, was Lloyd's agent in Scarborough and owned a small plantation, Franklyn's. He introduced cocoa and grapefruit cultivation to Tobago when the sugar markets collapsed. The small island was not the healthy paradise it was held to be in the handbook of the time; when the sixth child was born, Eliza and two children succumbed to 'black fever'. According to his obituary in 1927, Duncan made no fortune but grew wealthy 'in things that rusteth not' and lived long enough to hear that his grandson Colin, my father, had won the coveted Islands scholarship to Trinity College, Cambridge.

Duncan, born in 1847, was son of John M'Gillivray and Margaret, daughter of Charles Macarthur and Janet McHardy. Perhaps this is the Margaret who provides the female connection to the Dunmaglass family, for the oldest possession preciously kept after many moves was her father's commission, as though it was his ancestry that was somehow significant.

Margaret was one of the many children of Charles Macarthur, a gentleman officer in the Nairnshire volunteers, farmer, vintner and innkeeper at Cawdor. According to his gravestone, he was born in the 1760s, and according to his sword that is displayed at the Military Museum at Fort George, was of Polneach and Proaig (Islay). Polneach seems to have been the site of an 18th century distillery that today makes the world-famous Royal Brackla whisky, one of Scotland's finest. Charles could not have been son of John Macarthur and his wife Janet M'Gillivray as his birth predates their marriage contract of 1784. Charles had a brother John; it may be he who married Janet M'Gillivray. They seem to be the sons of Charles Macarthur and Jean Macpherson who lived at Torrich. In Polneach, at the same time as Charles, lived Peter Macarthur, who witnessed John Macarthur and Janet M'Gillivray's marriage contract with Farquhar of Dalcrombie, as well as John Macpherson of Killihuntly, cousin of John M'Intosh of Kyllachy. (Charles is mentioned in the Farr Manuscript for a previous marriage to May of the Corribrough M'Intoshes, whose father farmed at Auchindown in Cawdor, while Peter Macarthur's son Alexander married a sister).[107]

---

[107] Freemasonry in Inverness: John Tulloch was an unruly brother; one of his crimes was in 1756 having 'received, entered and admitted four apprentices without the advice and consent of the Master and Wardens.' John's friends were of good standing, being James

One M'Gillivray generation earlier was Duncan, dyer by trade, who worked the waulkmill at Cawdor. As well as supplying the distilleries for the whisky, the water from the river one day washed the linen, uniforms and blankets from Fort George. Marjory could trace the family no further back.

The old parish records that Marjory had not seen are now more accessible thanks to the Church of Latter Day Saints. Our M'Gillivrays can be traced through the parish registers to early 18th century and were known as M'Farquhar, perhaps grandsons of Farquhar McAllister of Dunmaglass, whose son also signed M'Farquhar. Farquhar M'Allister had acquired the deeds to Dunmaglass in 1626 and in exchange owed his feudal superior frequent attendance at Cawdor. Such a relationship is speculative but Duncan, dyer, was proud of the name: when his second child and first son was born, he was baptized under the name of M'Farquhar, and not M'Gillivray like an older sister. This is why the professional genealogists who helped Marjory had been unable to identify him.

In early 18th century, there were various M'Farquhars in Cawdor: John, Duncan and William, principal tenants in Reriach, Ballinryd and Glengoully. Our branch tenanted Reriach. 108 When good Sir Hugh Campbell died at in 1715, John M'Farquhar supplied the ox and cattle for the funeral feast.

As if two names were not enough, the M'Farquhars, alias M'Gillivrays, were M'Kerchars on the Cawdor rent-rolls. Both names mean son of Farquhar. Duncan's parents were Duncan M'Farquhar alias M'Gillivray, farmer in Reriach, and Janet Falconer from Nairn, who married in 1768.[109] When Duncan's Fraser cousin of Glengoully, son of William Fraser and Janet M'Gillivray of Reriach, had a first child, Duncan was godfather. Godparents to the second child were John Macarthur and his wife Janet M'Gillivray at the neighbouring farm of Achneim. This is the

---

McPherson in Calder, Donald McPherson, brother to Cluney, McIntosh of Corribrough and his brother-in-law, one McKerquhar.

[108] A M'Gillivray kilt was brought back to Reriach by a young herd lad from the battle fields of Culloden. Kenneth MacRae, *Northern Narrative*.

[109] Some time after this, the M'Farquhar's co-tenants at Reriach were Falconers who moved from Ardclach.

only instance that Janet is godmother while John at Achneim appears as godfather in the parish registers five times between 1788 and 1795, including to Charles Macarthur's son John. Was Janet, whether daughter or not of Jean and Duncan Roy, also a cousin of William Fraser and Duncan at Reriach?

Marjory searched for a Dunmaglass daughter, possibly a Margaret, with a Cawdor M'Gillivray spouse. There was no 18th century Margaret at either Dunmaglass or among our Cawdor ancestry - unless the Margaret on the Lagg stone was an ancestor and a Dunmaglass daughter.[110] The best-known Dunmaglass daughter who married another M'Gillivray was Jean Roy; but it is unlikely that Duncan in Reriach was her son. Yet there is a genetic clue to a possible link between the Reriach and Roy M'Gillivrays. William MacFarquhar and his wife Christian Campbell from Carnoch in the 1730s had two sets of twins, Donald and Duncan, and Donald and Farquhar, multiple births that do not recur in the Cawdor family and are seldom found among the Strathnairn M'Gillivrays. The twin gene, however, appears in the families we have been looking at: Lachlan, Indian trader, had twin grandchildren in America, William of Montreal had twin native sons - the twin gene was to continue - and his 'cousin' Neil John, grandson of Farquhar of Dalcrombie, also fathered twins. There may of course be others that have not been identified.[111]

---

[110] William MacGillivray in Auldearn thought the families were related; when Australian M'Gillivrays descendants of the Little Mills family visited, they also tried to locate the Cawdor M'Gillivrays.

[111] This is an interesting although not very reliable indicator because so few baptisms were registered. The Cawdor twins are the oldest reported; there were two or three M'Gillivray families with twins in Ardclach the next decade, and others thereafter; also David M'Gillivray with twins Charles and Ann in 1784 at Edinkilly, Moray. In April 2002, I was contacted by Catherine McTavish in America who had traced her family to her first Canadian ancestor, Donald McTavish, born in Boleskine, Inverness in November 1800. His marriage certificate showed him as son of Archibald McTavish and Mary M'Gillivray. There was the baptism of a Donald McTavish registered at the right period in Garthbeg, Boleskine; son of Archibald and Ann M'Gillivray. This Ann M'Gillivray was sister of William of the NWC. The error in the first name of the mother can be considered insignificant: each generation of American McTavishes had passed down the twin gene inherited from the Roy M'Gillivrays. Dr. Harry Duckworth, authority on the McTavishes, validates this lineage for Cathy.

At the farm of Bochrubin at the same time as Donald Roy, was Elspeth M'Gillivray who married Duncan M'Gruir and had twins born in 1778. The M'Gruirs, an uncommon name

An earlier 17th century Margaret, daughter of Farquhar M'Allister, married Alexander Macpherson of Crubenmore and Breakachie. The different Macphersons at Cawdor - James, factor to Lord Campbell, John at Polniach, Jean in Torrich and her son in Polniach - may have descended from this early Margaret, but such a connection would have been too distant to be meaningful in the Dunmaglass litigation. The villagers of Cawdor were, after the arrival of the Macphersons and M'Intoshes and a few generations of intermarriage, each connected to these old Highlander clansmen, the only significance for the Cawdor M'Gillivrays being that Dunmaglass in the 19th century was in search of a M'Gillivray owner.

In the mid 18th century, William M'Gillivray, schoolmaster at Cawdor, was son of either John and Janet M'Glashan in Reriach, William and Christian Campbell in Reriach, or John and Margaret McLean in Glengoully, the parents of a Lachlan born in early 1720. After the battle of Culloden, William moved to Dalmagarry as tacksman and innkeeper, taking over from Gillies McBean, a Battle of Culloden hero. William drew up the marriage contract of one of Dunmaglass' granddaughters, Emilia M'Intosh of Holm; his son or brother, Duncan, was godfather to Duncan, dyer, in 1777. Was this the Duncan who married Jean Roy? Little is known about Dalmagarry, except that the family seems to have continued there until the late 18th century when a document in the Dunmaglass papers states they were considered bankrupt. *Letters of Two Centuries* shows Mr. M'Gillivray at Dalmagarry as elder of the church, in charge of distribution of meal during the winter of the white pease. One of his sons, a blind William Jr., supplied dogs to Dunmaglass, and sued Colonel Thornton, an English sportsman touring the Highlands, for unpaid wages when he looked after a hunting lodge, 'Castle Thornton' at Aviemore, in his absence. There is a courteous note from Farquhar of Dalcrombie addressed to him, referring to mutual affairs that were before the courts in Inverness.

---

in Strathnairn, were claimed as ancestors by the Alabama M'Grews who also held they had a blood-tie with Alexander M'Gillivray, chief of the Creeks

I feel that all the possible relationships with the Dunmaglass family have been exhausted. The connection - should one exist - might not be so easily discernible.

However unsatisfying it is not to have lifted the veil on the secrets of the Dunmaglass family rather than describe them, the geographical and spiritual journey into the 'wild and majestic' 18th century Strathnairn has been worth the while, at times sombre and at others heart-wrenchingly humbling. There is every hope that this history will become clearer with time, with easier access to historical documents and still unopen repositories such as Cawdor Castle archives or with the finding of lost books or a chest with M'Gillivray documents like the one at Moy whose key was mislaid when Julia visited. There is also the possibility that old documents will be found in some dark corner in existing archives or carry fuller descriptions when indexed. So it is left to a yet undeclared M'Gillivray historian, genealogist and lover of old documents to be the 'servant of truth' and fill in the missing history of this 'minor' Highland clan.

(1) McPherson Muniments, NAS, Edinburgh. Dr. Alan G. Macpherson believes that she was probably past child-bearing age at the time of this marriage.

(2) After Alexander's death, Agnes married secondly William Forbes of Skellater, with issue. (One son, said to have been born about 1644, John Forbes of Inverernan, died a prisoner in Carlisle.) Alexander must therefore have died soon after his marriage.

(3) Sir Aeneas McPherson's Genealogy of the McPhersons shows she married Alexander McPherson of Crubenmore and Breakachie (Dr. Alan G. Macpherson). The Farr MS states she married Fraser of Meikle Garth.

(4) Eldest son in 1670

(5) Eldest son in 1681

(6) Title: Portioner of Dalcrombie or of Aberchalder

Note:

One of the earliest M'Gillivray wills is that of an Agnes Neyn James vick phail vick Conachy, given up in 1676 by her husband Alexander M'Gillivray in Dunmaglass. This Agnes is presented in the litigation papers as being the wife of Alexander of Dunmaglass, but this does not seem possible as Alexander is reportedly deceased some thirty years earlier. This Alexander's mother is named as Euphan Steuart, and he has a brother John.

175

TABLE 2: THE M'GILLIVRAYS IN LONNIE AND CANADA

DONALD THE TUTOR (Portioner of Dalcrombie)
b abt 1623; m MARIE M'INTOSH OF CONNAGE; dd by 1676

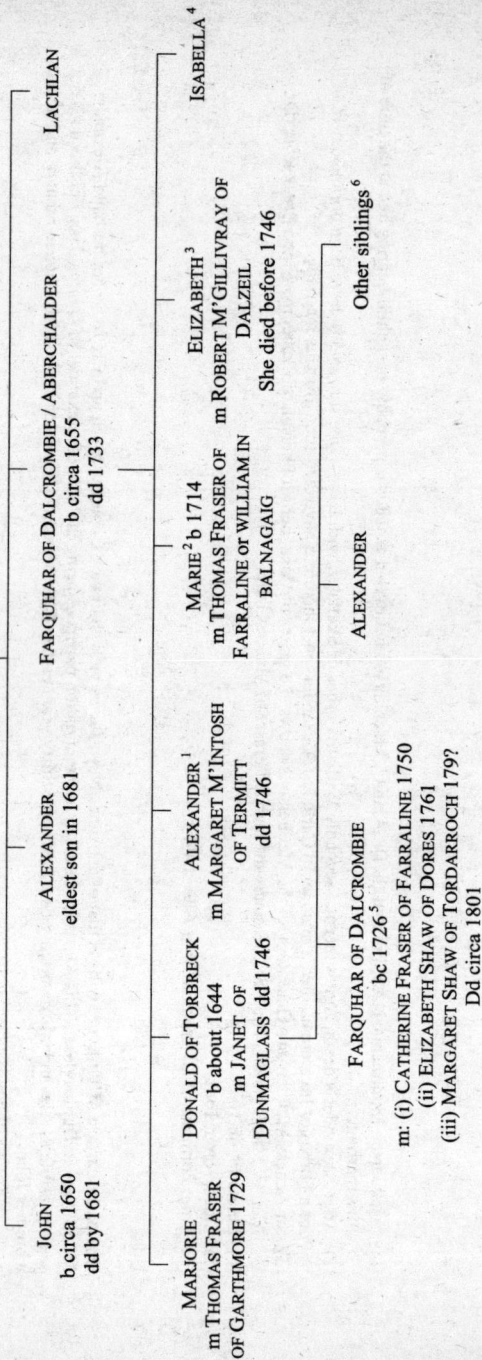

JOHN
b circa 1650
dd by 1681

ALEXANDER
eldest son in 1681

FARQUHAR OF DALCROMBIE / ABERCHALDER
b circa 1655
dd 1733

LACHLAN

MARJORIE
m THOMAS FRASER
OF GARTHMORE 1729

DONALD OF TORBRECK
b about 1644
m JANET OF
DUNMAGLASS dd 1746

ALEXANDER[1]
m MARGARET M'INTOSH
OF TERMITT
dd 1746

MARIE[2] b 1714
m THOMAS FRASER OF
FARRALINE or WILLIAM IN
BALNAGAIG

ELIZABETH[3]
m ROBERT M'GILLIVRAY OF
DALZEIL
She died before 1746

ISABELLA[4]

FARQUHAR OF DALCROMBIE
bc 1726[5]
m: (i) CATHERINE FRASER OF FARRALINE 1750
(ii) ELIZABETH SHAW OF DORES 1761
(iii) MARGARET SHAW OF TORDARROCH 179?
Dd circa 1801

ALEXANDER

Other siblings[6]

A genealogical chart:

MARGARET – ALEXANDER (ALEXR died circa 1815)

Children:

- JANET m MICHAEL M'GILLIVRAY in Inverness
- ISABELLA m DONALD FRASER OF BALLOAN
- WILLIAM b circa 1762
- LACHLAN
- JOHANNA b circa 1784 m ALEXR DALLAS in 1800; dd 1809
- DONALD IN DRUMBOY
- JOHN b circa 1771; m ISOBEL MCLEAN dd 1855
- DUNCAN?

Children of JOHANNA: FARQUHAR ELIZABETH

Children of JOHN: NEIL JOHN b 1827; m CATHERINE McDONELL

- MARY AUGUSTA b 4.2.1864
- JOHN WILLIAM b 4.2.1864
- ANGUS b 1867

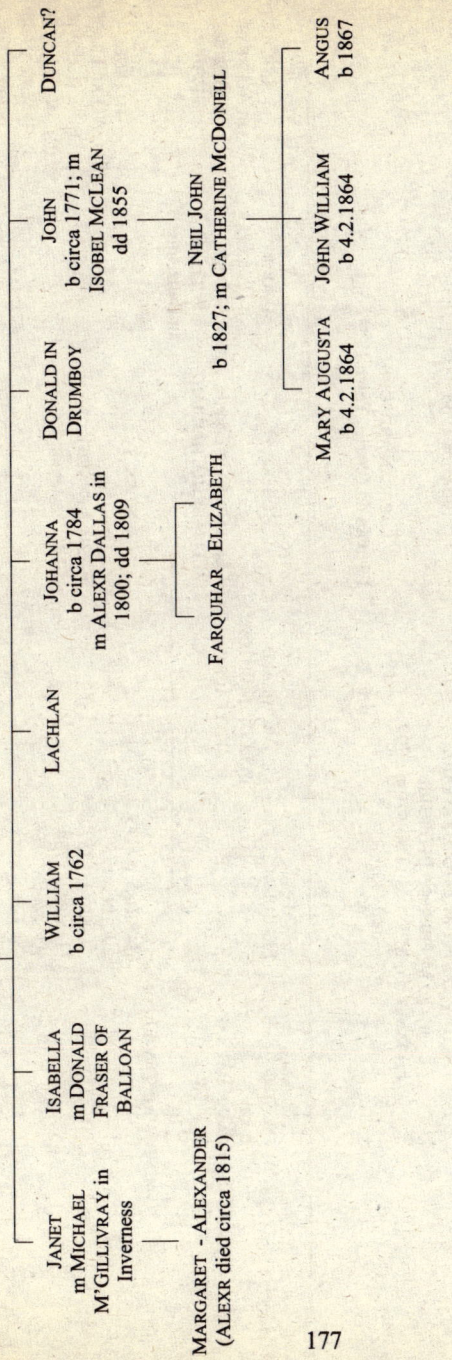

(1) The names of any issue are not known
(2) Marie's birth is registered in the parish records. A Mary, 'daughter to Dalcrombie' married Thomas Fraser of Farraline in Dunlichity in 1747 (OPR). This may not be the correct Dalcrombie family.
(3) Elizabeth died shortly afterwards; Robert remarried Elizabeth Chapman and a daughter served heir to her mother circa 1805
(4) Farr MS gives session records as source for her death in 1709
(5) Farr MS states he joined the 1745-6 rebellion aged 19, putting his date of birth at 1726-7
(6) One daughter married a Mr. Grant

TABLE 3: THE M'GILLIVRAYS IN DALZEIL, AMERICA AND JAMAICA

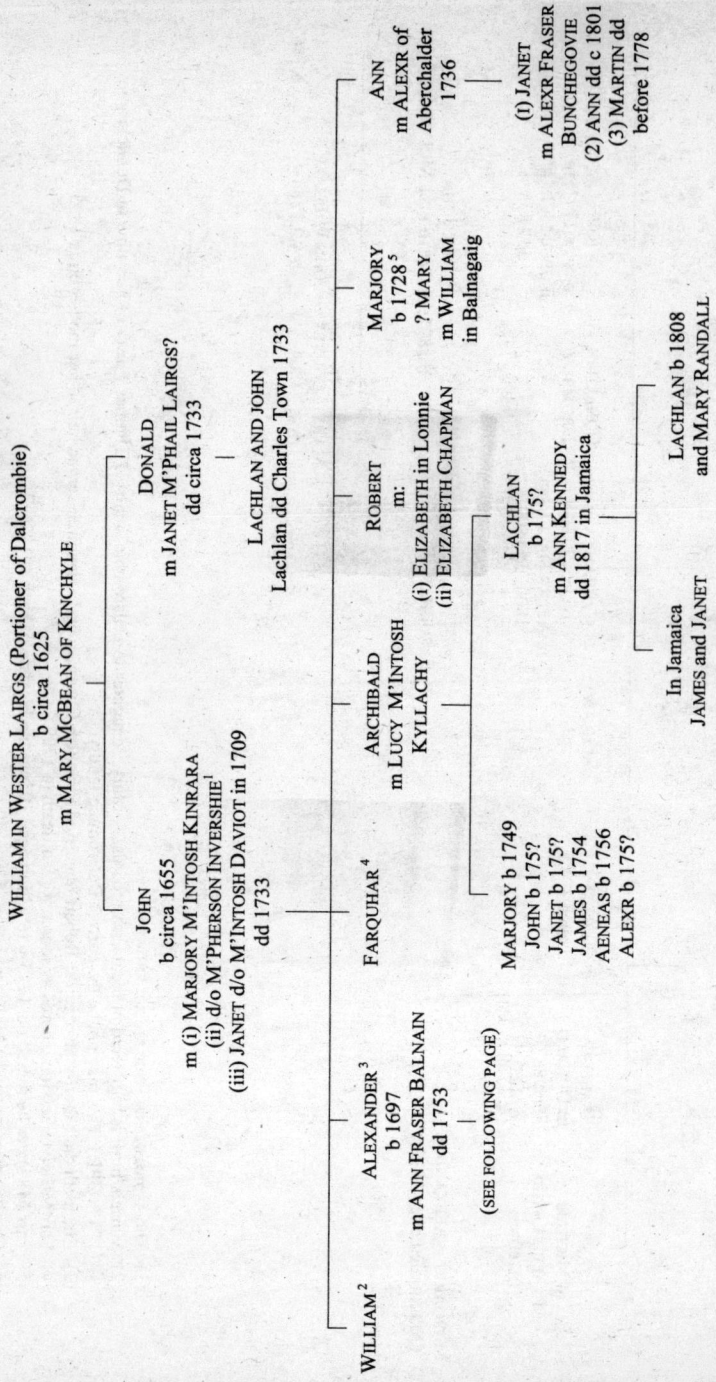

WILLIAM IN WESTER LAIRGS (Portioner of Dalcrombie)
b circa 1625
m MARY MCBEAN OF KINCHYLE

JOHN
b circa 1655
m (i) MARJORY M'INTOSH KINRARA
(ii) d/o M'PHERSON INVERSHIE[1]
(iii) JANET d/o M'INTOSH DAVIOT in 1709
dd 1733

DONALD
m JANET M'PHAIL LAIRGS?
dd circa 1733

LACHLAN AND JOHN
Lachlan dd Charles Town 1733

ANN
m ALEXR of Aberchalder
1736

MARJORY
b 1728[5]
? MARY
m WILLIAM
in Balnagaig

(1) JANET
m ALEXR FRASER
BUNCHEGOVIE
(2) ANN dd c 1801
(3) MARTIN dd
before 1778

WILLIAM[2]

ALEXANDER[3]
b 1697
m ANN FRASER BALNAIN
dd 1753

(SEE FOLLOWING PAGE)

FARQUHAR[4]

MARJORY b 1749
JOHN b 175?
JANET b 175?
JAMES b 1754
AENEAS b 1756
ALEXR b 175?

ARCHIBALD
m LUCY M'INTOSH
KYLLACHY

ROBERT
m:
(i) ELIZABETH in Lonnie
(ii) ELIZABETH CHAPMAN

LACHLAN
b 175?
m ANN KENNEDY
dd 1817 in Jamaica

In Jamaica
JAMES and JANET

LACHLAN b 1808
and MARY RANDALL

ALEXANDER
(CONTINUED FROM PREVIOUS PAGE)

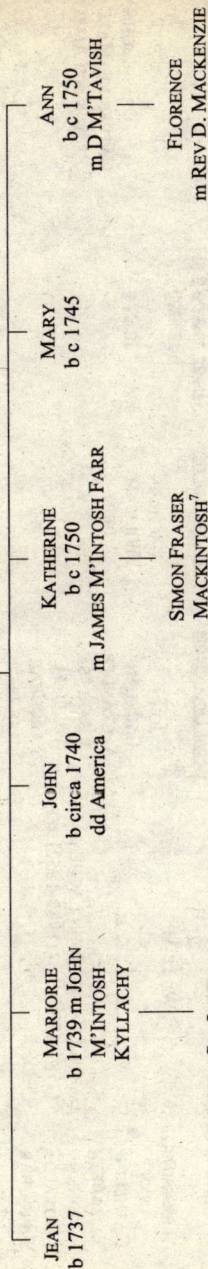

| JEAN b 1737 | MARJORIE b 1739 m JOHN M'INTOSH KYLLACHY | JOHN b circa 1740 dd America | KATHERINE b c 1750 m JAMES M'INTOSH FARR | MARY b c 1745 | ANN b c 1750 m D M'TAVISH |

SIR JAMES MACKINTOSH[6]

SIMON FRASER MACKINTOSH[7]

FLORENCE m REV D. MACKENZIE

(1) According to descendant, father of Alexander married a daughter of M'Pherson of Invereshie (See Table 5)
(2) Eldest son in 1709
(3) Eldest son in 1731. Robert was his brother-german
(4) Witness in 1717 and 1721
(5) Her baptism is in the OPR
(6) Two siblings
(7) Tenth child

179

TABLE 4: THE DUNMAGLASS FAMILY IN THE 18TH CENTURY

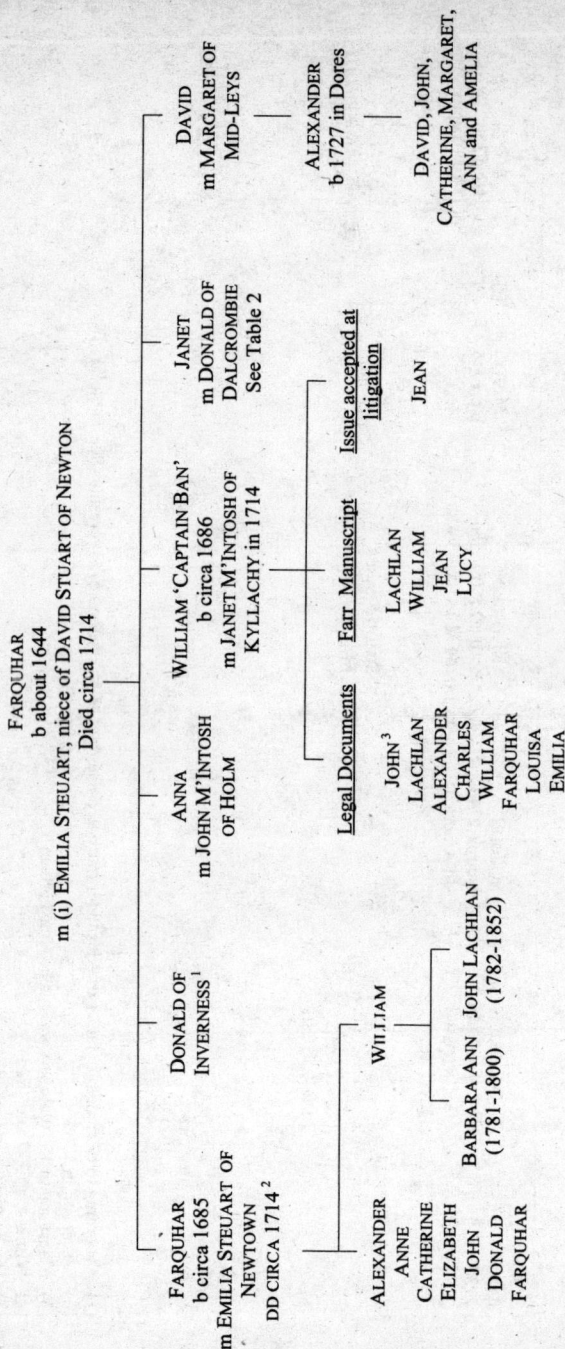

FARQUHAR
b about 1644
m (i) EMILIA STEUART, niece of DAVID STUART OF NEWTON
Died circa 1714

FARQUHAR
b circa 1685
m EMILIA STEUART OF
NEWTOWN
DD CIRCA 1714 [2]

DONALD OF
INVERNESS [1]

ANNA
m JOHN M'INTOSH
OF HOLM

WILLIAM 'CAPTAIN BAN'
b circa 1686
m JANET M'INTOSH OF KYLLACHY in 1714

JANET
m DONALD OF
DALCROMBIE
See Table 2

DAVID
m MARGARET
OF MID-LEYS

ALEXANDER
b 1727 in Dores

DAVID, JOHN,
CATHERINE, MARGARET,
ANN and AMELIA

ALEXANDER
ANNE
CATHERINE
ELIZABETH
JOHN
DONALD
FARQUHAR

WILLIAM

BARBARA ANN
(1781-1800)

JOHN LACHLAN
(1782-1852)

Legal Documents	Farr Manuscript	Issue accepted at litigation
JOHN [3]	LACHLAN	JEAN
LACHLAN	WILLIAM	
ALEXANDER	JEAN	
CHARLES	LUCY	
WILLIAM		
FARQUHAR		
LOUISA		
EMILIA		

(1) Donald had at least one daughter, Janet, as per the 1747 Inverness Deaths register

(2) Farquhar also had a natural daughter with Katherine Ross: Jean born in 1712 (she would not have been of child-bearing age when Jean Roy's daughters were born)

(3) Natural son John M'Gillivray; he married Isobel Fraser, SC29/10/420

180

TABLE 5: REVEREND DUNCAN MACKENZIE'S GENEALOGIES, 1849 (MURCHISON PAPERS, UNIVERSITY OF EDINBURGH)

(author's note: the layout has been simplified)

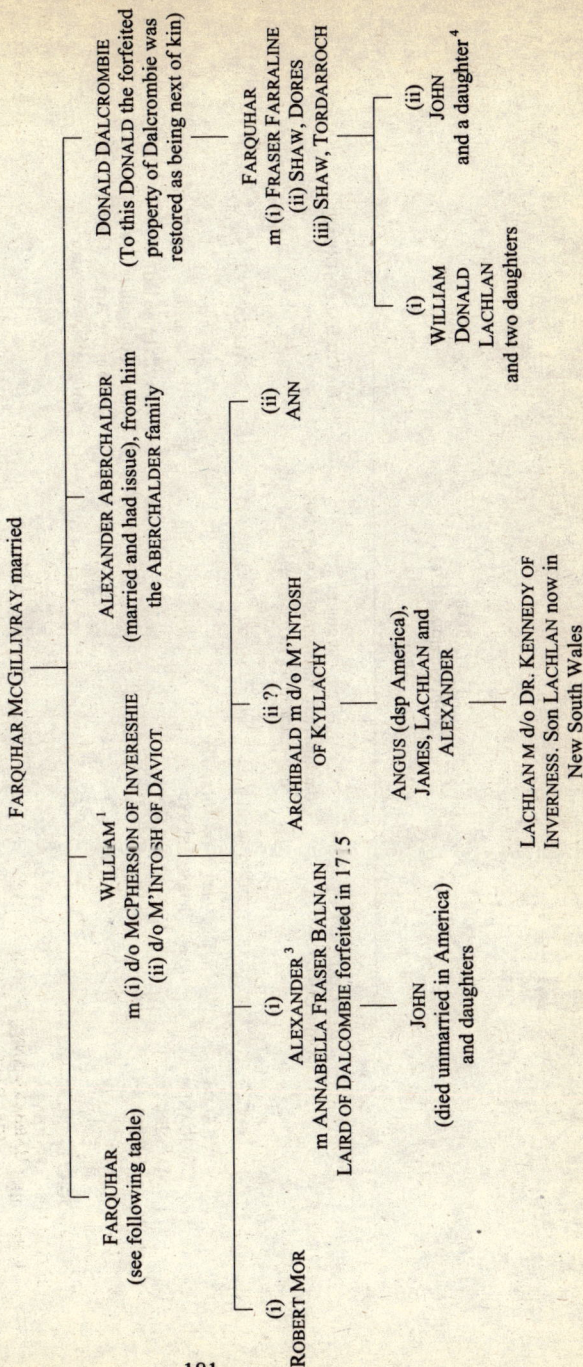

FARQUHAR McGILLIVRAY married

- FARQUHAR (see following table)
- WILLIAM[1] m (i) d/o McPHERSON OF INVERESHIE (ii) d/o M'INTOSH OF DAVIOT
  - (i) ROBERT MOR
  - (i) ALEXANDER[3] m ANNABELLA FRASER BALNAIN LAIRD OF DALCOMBIE forfeited in 17[ ]5
    - JOHN (died unmarried in America) and daughters
  - (ii?) ARCHIBALD m d/o M'INTOSH OF KYLLACHY
    - ANGUS (dsp America), JAMES, LACHLAN and ALEXANDER
    - LACHLAN M d/o DR. KENNEDY OF INVERNESS. Son LACHLAN now in New South Wales
  - (ii) ANN
- ALEXANDER ABERCHALDER (married and had issue), from him the ABERCHALDER family
- DONALD DALCROMBIE (To this DONALD the forfeited property of Dalcrombie was restored as being next of kin)
  - FARQUHAR m (i) FRASER FARRALINE (ii) SHAW, DORES (iii) SHAW, TORDARROCH
    - (i) WILLIAM DONALD LACHLAN and two daughters
    - (ii) JOHN and a daughter[4]

181

FARQUHAR
(from previous table)

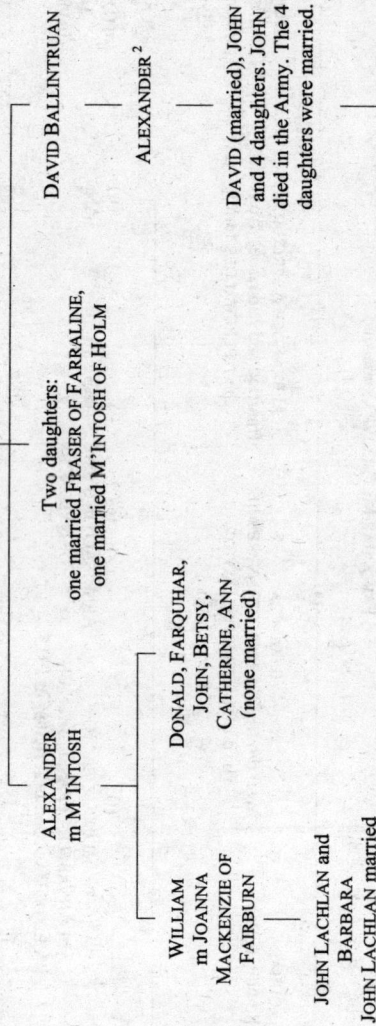

ALEXANDER
m M'INTOSH

Two daughters:
one married FRASER OF FARRALINE,
one married M'INTOSH OF HOLM

DAVID BALLINTRUAN

WILLIAM
m JOANNA
MACKENZIE OF
FAIRBURN

DONALD, FARQUHAR,
JOHN, BETSY,
CATHERINE, ANN
(none married)

ALEXANDER [2]

JOHN LACHLAN and
BARBARA
JOHN LACHLAN married
ELIZABETH WALCOT and
has no issue.

DAVID (married), JOHN
and 4 daughters. JOHN
died in the Army. The 4
daughters were married.

DAVID'S SON. Either he or
his father was a
gunsmith or armourer in Edinburgh and
afterwards in Liverpool.

The following has been noted at the bottom of the page: Copy Genealogical tree of the MacGillivrays of Dunmglass made up by the Revd. Duncan Mackenzie, Episcopal minister at Tullich, Strathnairn, from the information of his mother in law, Mrs. McGillivray or McTavish, who was born at Fort Augustus and died at Brin Cottage, and of her daughter, his own wife. The original is marked on the back thus: "To be kept safe, 1849 (signed) D. McKenzie"

Rev. Mackenzie writes:

(1) William married a daughter of Invereshie and had issue (i) Robert Mor who was killed at the battle of Culloden while leading on the M'Intosh Regiment (unmarried) and (ii) Alexander. Married 2dly a daughter of M'Intosh of Daviot, issue Archibald and Ann. (author's note: Robert's role at Culloden was also misreported by *The Inverness Courier* in the 19th century)

(2) The Rev. D. Mackenzie's wife recollects to have seen this Alexander at Balintruan where he died

(3) Alexander was the laird of Dalcrombie until his estate was forfeited in 1715. The property was restored to Donald, 3rd son of Farquhar chief, being the next of kin. This Alexander, by his daughters, was grandfather of the present Colonel Mackintosh of Farr and of the Revd Duncan Mackenzie's wife

(4) It is believed all the issue of the above parties (i.e. from this line of Dalcrombie) are now extinct.

Author's notes:

a) The further up the tree, the more inaccurate these genealogies clearly become, not matching archived deeds. However, note the inexplicable absence of William, the Captain Ban, Lachlan, Indian trader, and Jean. The latter two were alive during John Lachlan's childhood.

b) Note this table shows that the Ballintruan family is heir to Dunmaglass, or failing, Rev. Lachlan.

c) Note Alexander in Knocknageil has McPherson ancestor (Invereshie); there is a 1727 marriage in the Petty register of Alexander M'Gillivray in Dalzeil to a Margaret McPherson in mid-Coul. Perhaps a first marriage?

183

TABLE 6: THE M'GILLIVRAYS OF ABERCHALDER

MARTIN (MOR) M'GILLIVRAY in Aberchalder
m KATHERINE M'GILLIVRAY OF DUNMAGLASS about 1653

DONALD younger of Aberchalder circa 1688 dd by 1707

? —— ELIZABETH
m WM FRASER, Gortuleg
Dores parish register 1750

? WILLIAM – perhaps went to America – remembered by ARCHIBALD OF DAVIOT [1]

?

ALEXANDER
m ANN M'GILLIVRAY
d/o deceased JOHN IN DALZEIL in 1736
He died before 1774

ANNE
died circa 1801 [2]

MARTIN
succeeded in 1774
dd shortly thereafter

Heir male to ABERCHALDER in Carolinas; alive in 1779; known to WILLIAM OF DUNMAGLASS

?

JOHN
(a JOHN OF ABERCHALDER was enrolled in the University of Aberdeen in 1719)

JANET b 1742
m in 1769 CAPTAIN ALEXANDER FRASER OF BUNCHEGOVIE (1727-1814)
dd 1791

THOMAS
1769 - 1839

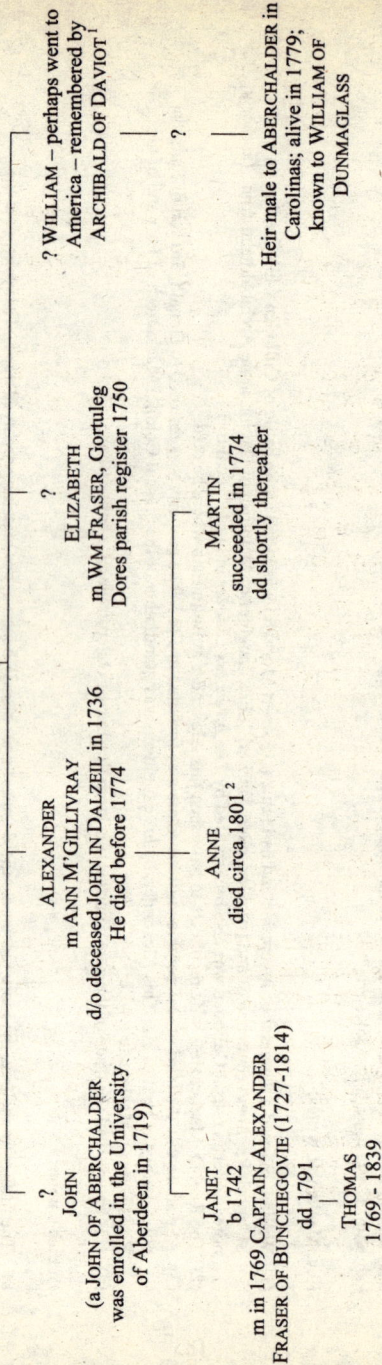

(1) For possible Williams in Carolina, consult *The McGillivray and McIntosh Traders on the Old Southwest Frontier, 1716-1815* by Amos Wright. This may not be the right position for William; he could be brother or nephew of Donald.

(2) Anne's heirs were: a) Alexander M'Gillivray in Daviot, her maternal cousin b) Alexander M'Gillivray coppersmith (husband of Marjory, Lachlan's niece) c) Donald Roy M'Gillivray in Dalscoilt who may have been another maternal cousin and b) Lt John and Mrs Ann Fraser in Errogie. Her nephew Thomas Fraser would inherit Alexander in Daviot's portion if the latter died before Anne.

Note: Farquhar of Aberchalder (grandfather of Farquhar of Dalcrombie) took the name Aberchalder not because he was a member of this family but because he had a legal lien on the property at the beginning of the 18th century.

SOURCES

BAIN, GEORGE. *History of Nairnshire*. Nairnshire Telegraph, Nairn 1893

BAIN, GEORGE. *The Lordship of Petty*. Nairnshire Telegraph, Nairn 1926

BAIN, GEORGE. *History of the Parish of Auldearn*. Nairnshire Telegraph, Nairn 1898

BEATTIE, ALASTAIR G. and MARGARET H. *Inverness District East, Monumental inscriptions pre-1855*. The Scottish Genealogy Society, 1996

BRADFORD, E. F. *MacTavish of Drunardy*. Whitby, 1991

BUNKLE, P. *Women's Suffrage, Kate Sheppard*. Broadsheet, Sept 1981

CAMPBELL, MARJORY WILKINS. *McGillivray, Lord of the Northwest*. Clarke, Irwin & Company Limited, Toronto, Vancouver 1962

CASHIN, EDWARD J. *Lachlan McGillivray, Indian Trader, The Shaping of the Southern Colonial Frontier*. The University of Georgia Press, 1992

CRAVEN, J. B (editor). *Journals of the Episcopal Visitations of the Right. Rev. Robert Forbes 1762 & 1770*. Skeffington & Son, London, 1886

FORBES, DUNCAN. *Culloden Papers: Comprising an Extensive and Interesting Correspondence from the Year 1625 to 1748*. London. T. Cadwell and W. Davies, 1815

FRASER-MACKINTOSH, CHARLES. *Minor Septs of Clan Chattan: An Account of the Confederation of Clan Chattan - Its Kith and Kin*. John Mackay, Glasgow, 1898

FRASER-MACKINTOSH, CHARLES. *Letters of Two Centuries chiefly connected with Inverness and the Highlands, from 1616 to 1815*. A. & W. Mackenzie, Inverness, 1890.

GORDON, REV. ALEXANDER. The United Parishes of Daviot and Dunlichity. In Sir John Sinclair, ed., *The Statistical Account of Scotland*. 27:54-64. 20 vols. East Ardsley, Wakefield, Eng. E. P. Publishing, 1981

HANCOCK, DAVID. *Citizens of the World, London Merchants and the Integration of the British Atlantic Community, 1735-1785*. Cambridge University Press, 1995

INNES, COSMO (editor). *The Book of the Thanes of Cawdor*. 1859

INNES, SIR THOMAS (Lord Lyon of Arms, KCVO, Advocate). *The Tartans of the Clans and Families of Scotland.* W & AK Johnston, Ltd, Edinburgh and London 1952

MACAULAY, THOMAS BABINGTON, BARON *Lord Macaulay's Essays and Lays of Ancient Rome: The Earl of Chatham, January 1834 and October 1844.* Longmans, Green and Co, London, 1920

MACKAY, WILLIAM (editor). *The Letter-book of Bailie John Steuart of Inverness, 1715-1752.* T. and A. Constable, Edinburgh, 1915

MACKENZIE, REVEREND DUNCAN. McGillivrays of Dunmaglass genealogy. 1849-1852, Murchison papers. University of Edinburgh Library MS 2262 '2'3

MACKINTOSH, CATHERINE. Correspondence. Manuscripts Department, National Library of Scotland, Ediburgh.

MACKINTOSH, ROBERT JAMES (editor). *Memoirs of Sir James Mackintosh.* London, Edward Moxon, 1836

MACKINTOSH, SIMON FRASER. Farr Manuscript. National Library of Scotland, Edinburgh.

MCGILLIVRAY, ROBERT, AND GEORGE B. MACGILLIVRAY. *A History of the Clan MacGillivray.* G. B. Macgillivray, Ontario, 1973

MCGILVRAY, ROY. *McGillivrays on the Scottish OPRs.* Privately published and on the web. www.magma.ca/~mkort/oprnames.htm

MACRAE, KENNETH ALASTAIR. *Highland Handshake.* Northern Chronicle, Inverness, 1954

MACRAE, KENNETH ALASTAIR. *Northern Narrative.* Moray Press. Edinburgh and London, 1955

O'LEARY, PATRICK. *Sir James Mackintosh, The Whig Cicero.* Aberdeen University Press, 1989

PATON, HENRY. *The Mackintosh Muniments, 1442-1820.* Edinburgh: Privately printed, 1903

PARKER, ANTHONY W. *Scottish Highlanders in Colonial Georgia, The Recruitment, Emigration, and Settlement at Darien, 1735-1748.* The University of Georgia Press, Athens and London, 1997

PREBBLE, JOHN. *Culloden.* Penguin, London, 1996

RALPH, ROBERT. *William MacGillivray.* The Natural History Museum, London HMSO, 1993

SCARLETT, META HUMPHREY. *In the Glens where I was Young.* Siskin, Moy, 1988

SHAW, ALEXANDER MACKINTOSH. *Historical Memoirs of the house and clan of Mackintosh and of the clan Chattan.* R. Clay, Sons and Taylor, London, c1880.

THOMSON, DAVID. *Nairn in Darkness and Light.* Vintage, London, 1991

WRIGHT, AMOS. *The McGillivray and McIntosh Traders on the Old Southwest Frontier 1716-1815.* NewSouth Books, Alabama

Clan Chattan Association Journals, Edinburgh

Parish Records

Fraser-Mackintosh Collections, Inverness and Edinburgh

Inverness Archives

Session Court Cases, National Archives of Scotland, Charlotte Square, Edinburgh

Registries of Deeds, National Archives of Scotland, Princes Street, Edinburgh

Cases decided in the Court of Session. British Library, London

Papers of the McGillivrays of Dunmaglass. National Archives of Scotland

Scottish Notes & Queries. Editor John Bulloch, Aberdeen

Inverness Courier. Inverness Library

Public Records Office, Kew

McGillivray file. Lord Lyon Office, Edinburgh

Celtic Monthly (Volume 7)

The Encyclopedia of Canada. Volume IV (McGillivray). Editor W. Stewart Wallace. Toronto, 1936

Burke's Landed Gentry. Peerage Ltd. London

INDEX